"Zachary Petit is the best editor I have ever worked for. *The Essential Guide to Freelance Writing* is as brilliant, incisive, and thorough as I expected. Do everything he says for a more successful career!" —Susan Shapiro, *New York Times* bestseller and award-winning journalism professor

"As both freelance writer and magazine editor, Zachary Petit has put together the finest (and most amusing) book I've read on how to break into professional writing and what to do once you get in the door. Funny, inspiring, and brimming with crucial nuts-and-bolts information, *The Essential Guide to Freelance Writing* should be on every freelancer's bookshelf." —Melissa Rossi, former travel columnist and author of the What Every American Should Know series.

"Want to score more writing gigs and earn well while doing what you love? Here's your chance to learn the ins and outs of freelance writing from an actual editor and long-time writer who has seen it all—from difficult sources to snooze-worthy queries. Zachary's book offers new writers insider tips, counterintuitive advice (that works!), and a few naughty words (c'mon, you know they're funny)." —Linda Formichelli, co-author of *Write Your Way Out of the Rat Race ... and Step Into a Career You Love* and co-owner of The Renegade Writer Blog and UsefulWritingCourses.com

"Getting started as a freelance writer can seem like a daunting game: so much information to sort through and so many rules and stumbling blocks that seem designed to keep you out. Zachary Petit knows all about it, and that's why he wrote this book. It's blessedly simple, yet packed with all the information you need to figure out your own unique path into this business. Zac's hard-won wisdom is both educational and entertaining. *The Essential Guide to Freelance Writing* can save you tons of time, help you earn more money, and keep you out of trouble while you're doing it. If you grab a copy and read it, you'll be well equipped to dive into the wonderful, lively, rewarding world of freelance writing." —Elizabeth Sims, prize-winning novelist, contributing editor for *Writer's Digest*, and author of *You've Got a Book in You: A Stress-Free Guide to Writing the Book of Your Dreams.*

"Zachary Petit's *The Essential Guide to Freelance Writing* is exactly that: essential. Covering every topic a freelancer might need to understand, from query letters to tax deductions, Petit has created a veritable freelancer's bible of insight and wisdom, replete with concrete examples. Suited for both the emerging writer hoping to break into the market and the trained veteran looking for a useful reference, *The Essential Guide to Freelance Writing* is a must-have for independent writers. One wonders how we have survived for so long without such a volume." —Jacob M. Appel, author of *Einstein's Beach House*

THE ESSENTIAL GUIDE TO FREELANCE WRITING

HOW TO WRITE, WORK, & THRIVE ON YOUR OWN TERMS

ZACHARY PETIT

WD
WRITER'S DIGEST
BOOKS

WritersDigest.com
Cincinnati, Ohio

For more resources for writers, visit www.writersdigest.com/books.

19 18 17 16   5 4 3 2

Distributed in Canada by Fraser Direct
100 Armstrong Avenue
Georgetown, Ontario, Canada L7G 5S4
Tel: (905) 877-4411

Distributed in the U.K. and Europe by F+W Media International
Brunel House, Newton Abbot, Devon, TQ12 4PU, England
Tel: (+44) 1626-323200, Fax: (+44) 1626-323319
E-mail: postmaster@davidandcharles.co.uk

Distributed in Australia by Capricorn Link
P.O. Box 704, Windsor, NSW 2756 Australia
Tel: (02) 4577-3555
Library of Congress Cataloging-in-Publication Data

ISBN13: 978-1-59963-905-5

Edited by **RACHEL RANDALL**
Designed by **ALEXIS BROWN**
Production coordinated by **DEBBIE THOMAS**

 # DEDICATION

To my mentor, **MARC ALLAN**, the only cheerleader I had for a very long time

To the ethical **CHARLES ST. CYR**

And to **MIKE REDMOND**, who said, "Brand of the beer, name of the dog," and suddenly, it all clicked …

TABLE OF CONTENTS

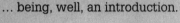

BY WAY OF INTRODUCTION

"Journalism is literature in a hurry."

—MATTHEW ARNOLD

I had a problem. A grave problem. An existential disaster requiring careful analysis and meditation. But I was in high school at the time, so I just muttered a few obscenities into the coffee I was drinking to look cool and went back to my Bukowski book.

I didn't know it back then, but I was confronting a common curse bestowed upon many an aspiring scribe: I knew I wanted to write. I knew I *had* to write. But I had no way to prove that I could actually do it.

All I had at the time was badly written music reviews for the high school newspaper I edited and a spectacularly large cache of poetry that is now hidden under my childhood bed at my parents' house, where it (thankfully, truly thankfully) can't find its way to the Internet.

I wanted to be a novelist, and I figured a sound career path would be to apply to college for journalism and write for newspapers like all my heroes did (Hemingway, Hunter S. Thompson, Twain, and, seemingly, everyone else). Thus I'd be able to make a living by writing nonfiction in some newsroom or another, while writing fiction on the side. After that, I'd become a best-selling novelist, and so on and so forth.

The more I dug in and learned, though, the more the nonfiction world at large seemed to be teeming with barriers and catch-22s. How could you break into writing for publications if you had no writing to show for yourself, only a feeling, a knowing?

It all seemed absurd, nigh impossible. So into my for-show coffee I wept.

But like all writers, I had no choice. I knew this thing was inside me and that the only logical way to avoid living my life with a used car salesman's sense of fulfillment was to follow it. I believe that we have no choice but to do what we do. So we keep trying at it until we break the glass barrier, or at least begin to scratch its surface.

In my case, I got accepted into journalism school. I wrote for the school newspaper and tried my hand at some feature stories; wrote some movie reviews, op-eds, and event recaps; and even continued writing my (praise God, not online) poetry for a bit. One Journalism 101 teacher flat out told me to quit because she didn't think I had the chops. I didn't take her advice: It was becoming clear to me that I got a thrill out of writing nonfiction, even if I wasn't any good at it yet. It made me feel electric. It made me feel alive. The real world is imbued with amazing and terrifying and hilarious and strange stories, and people will *pay* you to write about them. What writer wouldn't want to do that? Moreover, magazines offered a venue that equally favored creativity and storytelling alongside the principles of reportage found in newspapers. I was sold. I wanted to write nonfiction that read like fiction.

So I applied for fellowships and programs at a handful of prestigious schools and societies. I didn't get them. The writing world, again, seemed like an exclusive club—one that, at times, didn't even seem worth all the trouble. (Get ready for an introductory salary equivalent to what you made working as a cashier at Toys "R" Us last summer!)[1]

But, eventually, I caught a break (as we all do, if we keep at it long enough): *National Geographic* magazine hired me as an intern. They even gave me a shot at a small article for the print edition, which made my life when it came out. (I sometimes wonder if I should have called it

---

1 Don't tell anyone, but I made as much in my first reporter job as I did selling Barbies under the looming specter of a giant smiling giraffe.

a day when I was nineteen.) While there, I asked a staff writer how to become a staff writer at a magazine like *National Geographic*. His advice: "Work for newspapers for ten years." It was like a journalistic boot camp, he said. It makes you fast. It teaches you to produce. It trains you to interview and read sources. And it begins to instill in you all the basic narrative elements inherent to magazine writing.

I figured, what the hell? I wanted to write for magazines, but if this guy said that's what I had to do, then that's what I had to do. So after I graduated I began applying for newspaper jobs.

Again, I got rejected. Or, more accurately, and perhaps marginally worse: I received *no response*. I queried paper after paper. From the swampy stretches of Beaumont, Texas, to the glacier-flanked town of Juneau, Alaska, my résumé rode the rails of a country on an economic downturn alongside innumerable fellow bindle stick-toting candidates. The newspaper industry was teetering its way to its own obituary pages. I imagined scores of journalism grads like myself sitting at their parents' Compaqs, Sallie Mae looming over their shoulders, all in a cut-throat battle for the same hilariously tiny pool of bad-paying jobs.

After giving up on competitive metropolitan markets, I began targeting a paper in Northern Ohio. I e-mailed the editor to follow up on my résumé. No response. I called the editor. I harassed the editor. I begged the editor. Finally, either recognizing my bulldog, reporter-worthy tenacity, or simply succumbing to it, he conceded and offered me an interview. I drove three-and-a-half hours past endless cornfields and attempted to convince him of my passion, despite my lack of stellar clips. I got the gig. I moved into the second floor of a dilapidated mansion that was decades past its prime.

What followed was one of the greatest years of my life. The editors didn't seem to care too much what I wrote, so long as it filled pages and didn't result in a lawsuit, so I wrote everything I'd always wanted to— narrative features, news, Q&As, investigative pieces. I went on drug raids. I roamed prisons and abandoned schools that were allegedly haunted. It was everything I'd hoped and imagined journalism would be: life as adventure, simply waiting for someone to document it.

I built up a clip portfolio. From my crumbling Victorian and my dying laptop, I lived like a king on $18,000 a year. I'd finally been given a chance to prove that I could do what I always knew I could do.

Later, I took a job as a staff writer at an alt-weekly and eventually caught wind of an opening for a managing editor at *Writer's Digest*, the longest-running and biggest publication in the world for writers.[2] Starstruck, I figured that while I was vastly underqualified for such a gig, I'd hate myself if I didn't at least throw my hat in the ring. (Interview writers all day long? Yes. Yes, please.)

In the interview, I told the editor at the time, Maria Schneider, that while I didn't have a lot of editing experience (read: close to none), I knew I could do it. And, moreover, I was a writer. Wasn't that more important for a staff member at *Writer's Digest*? She asked me who my favorite author was. I said Vonnegut. We clicked. To this day, I still credit Vonnegut (and Maria) for launching my magazine career.

But let's stop for a moment and address the seeming narcissist in the room: What's the point of all this rambling?

To me, instructional books often read like a dry oration from a man behind the curtain. You don't know who that person really is. He speaks from a perceived podium of authority, cloaking the failures and rejections that truly made him who he is while proselytizing a set of best practices gleaned from an invisible pool of unspoken experience.

I want you to know how many times I have failed.

Writing is not easy. It's never easy. It's all about passion. You can never reach too high. Rejection happens, constantly. It's inherent to the field. It'll happen to you. But it doesn't mean anything. It'll make you sharper. It'll make you angrier. It'll draw the best out of you.

Moreover, my story is an example of one of many paths. The great beauty of writing is that everyone gets there in their own way. You don't have to do what I did, or what anyone else did. Just as you have your own writing method, everyone reaches their goals in a way that only they could have done. You are never too young or too old. You need

---

2 Note: This is not a shameless plug for the publisher of this book—I've read *Writer's Digest* magazine and Writer's Digest Books since high school.

4

no formal schooling. You need no literary pedigree. (My family is in the medical field; I'm a literary bastard and proud of it.)

When I was starting out, I searched for a book like this on magazines and the freelance world, and found none. That's why I pitched it to WD. Using honest insights from my years as a magazine editor, a staff writer, and a freelance writer, I want to present to you the fundamentals of the craft and a set of best practices for writing for publications, regardless of whether you want to do it full-time, part-time, or simply on occasion to get some good nonfiction credits to promote your fiction. The end result is your decision. The important thing to know is that there *is* a starting point—and that anyone can get there.

Freelancing is one of the greatest things on Earth.[3]

And, as I said before, many of us have no choice but to write.

It's time to prove you can do what you know you can do.

If you've got that itch inside of you, it's time to scratch it.

Here's how to freelance and get your words published.

—Zachary Petit, Cincinnati, 2015

---

[3] No dress code! No employees! Make your own hours! For more musings on the awesomeness of freelancing, visit writersdigest.com/essential-guide-to-freelance-writing and read the article "10 Reasons the Freelance Life Is a Good Life" by Art Spikol.

CHAPTER 1

BATTLING—AND BESTING—THE BASICS

"It's none of their business that you have to learn to write. Let them think you were born that way."

—ERNEST HEMINGWAY

"In the English language, it all comes down to this: Twenty-six letters, when combined correctly, can create magic."

—JOHN GROGAN

When it comes to writing, as with most things, starting is the worst part. Always. It's excruciating. Starting a query, starting an article, starting a poem, starting a book—even this book!—takes a leap of faith.

It takes courage. Trust your talent and your muse, and know that once you've formed a snowball, it'll begin to roll. And who knows, with luck, it'll turn into an avalanche.

It's easy and fun to dream, but starting is a whole other beast.

So, let's start.

DEFINING FREELANCING

Freelancing can seem like a vague activity and profession, often because people use the singular term to encapsulate any number of writing gigs and careers. Even after I'd been working as a reporter and staff writer for a while, I was still perplexed by freelancing—how people did it, how they got the "in" with a publication, how people made a sustainable income doing it. I had stringers writing for me when I was a weekly newspaper editor, but they were working for beans, and they'd been writing for the paper longer than I'd been there, so I had no clue how they found their way into my pages in the first place. I accepted their magical presence but never took the time to find out how they actually got their feet in the door. (Perhaps I was preoccupied by panic attacks and acid reflux spawning from my eight-feature-stories-a-week quota.)

Simply put (and obviously put), freelancing is when you, as a nonemployee of a company, write something for someone else's publication.[1] But it gets more complex, especially on the giving-advice side, when you take into account the degree to which one freelances or wants to freelance. Before we go any further, let's break down the different breeds of freelance writers so you can begin to form a picture of where you want to fall on the spectrum and what you want to accomplish.

---

1 I know, I know, it seems too early in this book for disclaimers. But it's worth noting as early as possible that when I ramble about freelancing for "publications," I actually mean *any* market, from traditional print outlets to their online counterparts to online-only outlets. This is due in part to highly imprecise language and industry jargon. But know that when a distinction is important, I'll make it. Moreover, when I say "freelancing," I'm generally referring to freelancing in the classic sense: editorial freelancing—writing for newspapers, magazines, and the like.

THE PART-TIME MAGAZINE FREELANCER

This is the category I fall into (and, to be honest, the one in which I've always felt most comfortable). Part-timers cover an amazingly (and often absurdly) diverse swath of day jobs and after-hours writing pursuits. I know writers who teach English classes during the day and write for video game blogs at night. I know writers who run fitness companies nine to five and pen literary criticism in their spare hours. In my day job, I'm the editor of *Print*, a highbrow newsstand magazine about the intersections of graphic design and visual culture. By night, I'm often writing about dinosaurs and other wonders for *National Geographic Kids*. (The two jobs occupy opposite ends of the spectrum but are equally thrilling.)

You can be a garbage truck driver and a freelancer. A college student and a freelancer. A lawyer and a freelancer. A lumberjack and a freelancer.

Those of us who go about the profession this way do so for a variety of reasons—to have another outlet for our writing, to pursue individual passions, to explore the nerdy topics that might not necessarily intersect with our day jobs, and to perhaps work toward being a full-time freelancer by slowly building a portfolio of clients and contacts over time.

Freelancing part-time is the best way to get started, versus plunging in headfirst full-time. Think of it like scuba diving. You probably want to take some lessons before hopping off the boat and fiddling with your breathing apparatus as sharks and stingrays glide by. On a practical level, if you have a day job, you'll have a guaranteed paycheck that will alleviate the lingering fear and desperation that comes with frantically trying to land assignments and articles before the gas gets shut off. When that burden is removed and you're free to explore the freelance world at your own pace, you can make steady, informed decisions about what you truly want to write about and who you truly want to write it for—versus having to slave away at an article for a business-to-business tax journal just to be able to afford McDonald's as a Friday night treat. I remain a part-time freelancer because, at this point in my

8

life, it lets me take on the assignments I *want* to take on and none of the articles about refrigerator motors.

On the downside: It takes a level of dedication and passion to tread to your computer after an eight-hour day of work and not feel like you're on your way to the gallows (read: Mondays). But in my experience, once I start writing, it's always worth it, and I always leave my computer feeling better than when I sat down.

(And, ultimately, I suppose, I'd rather be tired than broke.)

THE FULL-TIME FREELANCER

I'm not going to lie: Full-time freelancing, and especially full-time freelancing for magazines, can be tough. I don't know a single full-time freelancer who isn't top-notch at what they do. They're amazing writers. They're amazingly well connected. They're great salespeople, and, most important, fantastic at selling themselves. And they're *fast*. They possess a stunning efficiency and ability to do all of these things at a breakneck rate, and they consistently deliver—because if they don't, they can't put bread on the table, and editors won't work with them again.

It's an intense game that doesn't involve just sitting around and writing, because half of the full-time freelancer's time is spent pitching. As an editor, I can tell you that at every publication I've ever worked at, we get far more (an insane amount more) pitches than we'd ever be able to accommodate. It's easy being choosy as an editor, and the sharpest pitch wins the day—and the one hundred other contenders unfortunately go home empty-handed. A freelancer must always have another pitch loaded in the queue, ready to go, and knows that rejection is just part of the game.

All of this isn't to say that freelancing full-time is not possible—it's entirely possible. And those I know who do it love it. You just have to be extremely good at it and have the right personality to effectively hustle and deliver.

Full-time freelancers often offset the more fun and stimulating magazine features they do by writing the less-than-fun stuff (the role that many part-time freelancers' day jobs occupy). They are likely the ones writing the refrigerator motor copy—and they want to, for good reason. *That sort of thing pays.* One full-timer I know is often regarded for the writing he does for men's magazines—but he spends the bulk of his time writing anonymous white papers for big companies.

There are always two sides to every coin, after all.

If you can get a steady gig doing assignments that you don't love but that pay, it'll make up a chunk of income, and you can then focus on the more fun articles that you get a kick out of doing.

So which is better all around: part-time freelancing or full-time freelancing? There's no one-size-fits-all answer. Freelancing is a tailor-made profession. I have never been a full-time freelancer because I'm not a fan of the hustle and the uncertainty (and I like to edit to offset my writing time). But I know countless writers who adore the hustle and excel at it. You just need to figure out which type of writer you are.

KNOWING YOUR MARKETS

In the freelance world, you'll constantly hear chatter about "markets." But we're not talking about the weekly neighborhood farmer's stand or the recent surge of hipster homegrown veggie swaps. A market is essentially anywhere a freelance writer could land her work, be it a newspaper, magazine, trade journal, and on and on. We'll cover this in much greater detail in chapter five, but it's worth noting here that you generally sell articles for magazines and newspapers with pitches—a description of the piece you'd like to write—versus submitting the full piece up front.

Knowing your markets is key to successful freelancing—both in terms of knowing where your writing and interests would best fit and in knowing the full extent of publications available to pitch.

The Internet is full of talk (and has been for years) about the death of print. This is something I'm constantly asked at writers conferences, because it directly pertains to markets and the number of places a writer can pitch. *Is it even worth it to get into the game these days?*

My view (indulge me as I step onto my soapbox for a moment): There's really no way to know what will definitively happen, and anyone who is speculating is doing just that—speculating. You'll find loud voices on both sides of the aisle, and you'll find that they quite enjoy hearing themselves talk. Some publications are struggling because of the loss of Borders's and Barnes & Noble's newsstands, ad dollars going to the Web, and so on. But a healthy segment of the audience does not want to let print go. And even if this wasn't the case, there are a slew of digital outlets anyone can write for. A good editor and a good publication (be it digital or print) offer something readers can't get everywhere: quality, expertise, and curation. I think general-interest publications will continue to take the biggest hits and specialty publications will continue to thrive.

Moreover, one need only look at the numbers to grasp the amazing field of writing opportunities out there. As Samir Husni, a longtime industry expert known as "Mr. Magazine" reported, 234 new magazines launched in 2014—a 21-percent increase over 2013. Anyone who feels there is no place left to query needs to head over to the library or bookstore, or the website of their choice, to check out a market resource. Market books are the phone books of the writing world—and a crucial lifeline. Rather than Googling "good cooking magazines" or the like in search of markets, I've always preferred the writers market books because everything is located in one place, and you can quickly thumb through and flag the markets you think may be good homes for your work. You'll also find out how to submit, what types of pieces to submit, who to submit to, etc. It's a shortcut to everything you need to know to get in touch and get your pitch read.

There are a lot of such resources out there. I'm sure my editor would throw my book in the WD fireplace if I didn't mention the brand's *Writer's Market*. But, again, I do so not to shill for WD but because it's a fantastic resource that has been deemed "The Writer's Bible" and has helped countless famous scribes in their journey to becoming famous. (Stephen King calls it out in his essential *On Writing*.)

To give you a bird's-eye view of all the types of publications one can pitch, let's take a peek inside the table of contents of a market book. While we're at it, I'll offer some background and insight into the core markets.

CONSUMER MAGAZINES

Essentially these are what you think of when you think of "magazines"—publications found on newsstands and in specialty shops, and read by general consumers interested in the subject matter. They cover a vast array of topics (no matter what the subject, a magazine exists for it; at F+W, which publishes *Print*, there are magazines on everything from survivalist skills to knitting to numismatics to bow hunting to ice fishing).

If we crack into *Writer's Market*, here's a sampling of the categories we would find:

Animal
Art and Architecture
Associations
Astrology, Metaphysical, and New Age
Automotive and Motorcycle
Aviation
Business and Finance
Career, College, and Alumni
Child Care and Parental Guidance
Comic Books
Consumer Service and Business Opportunity
Contemporary Culture
Disabilities
Entertainment
Ethnic and Minority
Food and Drink
Games and Puzzles
Gay and Lesbian
General Interest
Health and Fitness
History
Hobby and Craft
Home and Garden
Humor
In-Flight (Note: big paychecks!)
Juvenile
Literary
Men's

Military

Music

Mystery

Nature, Conservation, and Ecology

Personal Computers

Photography

Politics and World Affairs

Psychology and Self-Improvement

Regional (think *Pittsburgh Magazine*, *Ohio Magazine*,
    Nevada Magazine)

Relationships

Religious

Retirement

Rural

Science

Sex

Sports (everything from skiing to martial arts to baseball)

Teen and Young Adult

Travel and Camping

Women's

TRADE JOURNALS

Ever hear writers talking about "technical markets" or "business-to-business" markets? They're more or less synonymous with trade journals—publications that serve a specific industry. As I noted earlier, trade journals may seem less sexy to write for than the big glossies, but this is where many a freelancer makes her bread and butter. The pay rates are often great because it takes a specialized knowledge and writer to be able to pull off the articles. (Subscription rates tend to be quite high for readers because the knowledge is so niche and hard to find at such a high level elsewhere—for instance, a subscription to *Publishers Weekly* will set you back $249.99.) Accessibility is also a bonus for these markets. While the editors of *Esquire* are drowning in queries, an editor for a trade journal that pays just as well doesn't have a line out the door of people who can write what she's looking for. A good starting point to consider: What is *your* specialty—and in which of these areas might you be able to offer some wisdom?

Advertising, Marketing, and PR

Art, Design, and Collectibles (Pitch me at *Print!*)

Auto and Truck

Aviation and Space

Beauty and Salon

Beverages and Bottling

Book and Bookstore

Brick, Glass, and Ceramics

Building Interiors

Business Management

Church Administration and Ministry

Clothing

Construction and Contracting

Drugs, Health Care, and Medical Products

Education and Counseling

Electronics and Communication

Energy and Utilities

Engineering and Technology

Entertainment and The Arts

Farm

Finance

Fishing

Florists, Nurseries, and Landscapers

Government and Public Service

Groceries and Food Products

Home Furnishings and Household Goods

Hospitals, Nursing, and Nursing Homes

Hotels, Motels, Clubs, Resorts, and Restaurants

Industrial Operations

Information Systems

Insurance

Jewelry

Journalism and Writing

Law

Lumber (... weird, right?)

Machinery and Metal

Maintenance and Safety

Management and Supervision

Marine and Maritime Industries

Medical

Music

Office Environment and Equipment
Paper
Pets
Plumbing, Heating, Air Conditioning, and Refrigeration
Printing
Professional Photography
Real Estate
Resources and Waste Reduction
Selling and Merchandising
Sport Trade
Stone, Quarry, and Mining
Toy, Novelty, and Hobby
Transportation
Travel
Veterinary

NEWSPAPERS

Ah, the humble newspaper. While I believe that print magazines will stick around for a while, newspapers are admittedly more challenged. Preferences in readership and digestion of news have fueled the changes, and many papers have gone under, shrunk their folios, adopted tabloid sizes, and, most tragically, cut down the size of their newsrooms. (Which takes a toll on the lives of staff writers, and, more crucially, the content of the news we're receiving. But that's a whole other book.)

The one upside is that newspapers utilize freelancers, and now they need them more than ever—especially to offset the quick-breaking news items, arrest reports, and wire stories that constitute the bulk of the paper.

Newspapers can be a great place to break in and build up some clips that you can parlay into magazine writing and other types of content. If you have a good story, a publication will often commission it, and one story often leads to many. The pay rates aren't great, but the exposure and clips can be, and if the staff is occupied with public meetings and other necessary areas of coverage, there's a high likelihood that the editors are looking for some meaty, more interesting features for the weekend edition.

Depending on where you live, here are some of the papers you might run into:

- **DAILIES:** Most cities have one (and in the past they probably had two). More often than not, they're owned by one of the big newspaper conglomerates (Gannett, E.W. Scripps Company, etc.).
- **COMMUNITY NEWSPAPERS:** Often released in a weekly format, these papers tend to cover suburban or other outlying areas, and are often owned by the same companies as the dailies, which sometimes publish their pieces (and vice versa).
- **ALTERNATIVE WEEKLIES:** Descendants of the 1960s counter-culture indie press, alt-weeklies operate on a free format and make their money in ad sales and classifieds. They're often no-holds-barred, in your face, and don't adhere to the shirt-and-tie aesthetic of daily newspapers. They're a direct counterpoint to the more mainstream publications and cover the gritty realities of a locale alongside hip restaurants, neighborhoods, etc. Again, they can be great sources of clips, but don't expect to earn more than the price of the meal at the restaurant you're reviewing. Large media companies also own a portion of the alt-weekly market, producing more reader-friendly—and family-friendly—publications.
- **NEWSLETTERS:** Let's add these here. (Hey, they're paper, right?) Newsletters cover the gamut, from religious organizations to community action teams, and can also be a good place to get a start. They have small circulations and even smaller paychecks, but they're worthwhile, especially if they jibe with your areas of interest.

ONLINE MARKETS

Ten years ago, my colleagues would have laughed at me behind my back—or, knowing my colleagues, to my face—if I'd included online markets in this book. Now, online markets are commonplace. Online markets can be fantastic for a writer.

At writers conferences, one of the questions most often posed to me is some variant of "If a writer has online clips but no print clips, should we send you links to them? Are online clips worth anything?"

Let it be said: Any editor who refuses to look at and/or acknowledge the merit of an online clip is stuck on old-school notions of print as the only arbiter of quality, and he is likely a curmudgeon (they're a dime a dozen in this business, and I look forward to fully evolving into one some day). Good writing is good writing, no matter whether it's on the back of a napkin or in *The New York Times*. Haters gonna hate, and gatekeepers gonna gate.[2][3]

Sure, there are wildly varying tiers of quality in online markets. For instance, The Huffington Post (which, amazingly, still does not pay writers, by the way) is greater than eHow.

There's *Salon.com*. *Slate*. And innumerable others. (At *Writer's Digest*, one of my duties was to manage the magazine's style guide. Our house style was to italicize the names of print publications and to simply uppercase the names of websites. But when many websites began surpassing the quality of some print publications, we decided it was time to change the style and to italicize the names of paying online magazines. A simple and small example in the larger microcosm of the media world, but an indicator of the paradigm shift that has been taking place over the last twenty years.)

And then, of course, nearly every print publication has an online counterpart—and breaking in on the Web is easier and often serves as a gateway to breaking into the hallowed print counterpart. While payment structures vary, you can probably expect to make less writing for a Web counterpart to a print magazine than for the print publication itself. At *Print* magazine, our Web stories (yes, ironically, we have them) pay 16 percent of what they would in the magazine. When I was at *Writer's Digest*, we didn't have an online budget. Again, writing for the street cred that many online outlets afford can be well worth your time.

---

2 E-mailing my editor right now to apologize in advance for this sentence.

3 Editor's note: In a rare instance of author and editor being on the same wavelength, I simultaneously approved this sentence and then made it far less grammatically sound, à la Taylor Swift.

I wasn't paid a dime for a *McSweeney*'s online piece I did, but you better believe I mention it in nearly every bio I publish.

So what about blogs, smaller unknown websites, and other digital outlets you feel are "lesser"? If an editor asks for clips and they're all you've got, send links to them—but only if you feel they exhibit the standard of quality you believe in. Again, good writing is good writing—and anything you can show an editor that displays your good writing is worth including.

CONTENT MILLS

Think of the content mill as a modern-day literary sweatshop—writers hunkering down at hot keyboards, plowing away at 3,000-word articles for, literally, pennies.

Content mills were born because someone figured out that by targeting popular search result terms, they could commission an army of crappy posts catering to these terms and dominate Google's results. (Remember when you'd search for something, and instead of a valid resource, you'd get fifty-six poorly written, untrue, bizarre, grammatical-mortal-sin-ridden pieces at the top of your results? Okay, yeah, so it still happens.)

I won't name names,[4] but here's the way these sites work: You write stories for either nothing or a low fee (like $15), and receive "affiliate" money (read: pennies) based on clicks. The company promises great exposure, experience, big checks if you get big clicks, etc. But in reality, most content mill writers work for beans and receive beans for affiliate cash—and for no real purpose. Editors won't be impressed by a piece (or several hundred) you did for one of these sites. They know the sites, who runs them, and the way they operate. You have a better chance of impressing this editor by sending a query written on the back of a liquor store receipt than you do writing for a content mill. You also won't learn anything from the editing. Many writers I've talked to

---

4 Ah, screw it, sure I will: Examiner.com, eHow, the dearly departed Suite101.com, claimer of many writerly souls, et al.

who have written for content mills lament the terrible editing and bad feedback (if any) they received.

Luckily, the scourge of content mills is marginally less prominent now than it was in its heyday in 2010, and fewer and fewer writers are falling for the gag.

Google has also wised up to what's been going on and changed their search algorithm, effectively scattering ant poison for the companies that were taking advantage of writers with honest aspirations and, in turn, misleading consumers. I'd advocate writing for nearly any market to gain experience—with the exception of this one.

So where should you pitch first? Newspapers? Magazines? Online markets? ~~Content mills?~~

Try not to think of it in singular terms. Envision all of these outlets and more as the canvas for your work. My best advice: Figure out the *types* of pieces that you want to write. (Essays? News articles? Profiles? Quizzes? Horoscopes?) Study all of the markets at your disposal. Then, pitch it or write it, no matter the venue. (Unless, of course, it's for a literary pyramid scheme.)

CHAPTER 2

IDEATION VACATION

"Ideas are like rabbits. You get a couple and learn how to handle them, and pretty soon you have a dozen."

—JOHN STEINBECK

"That's the great secret of creativity. You treat ideas like cats: You make them follow you."

—RAY BRADBURY

"The truth is, it's not the idea, it's never the idea, it's always what you do with it."

—NEIL GAIMAN

On the first day of my first newspaper job, I sat down at my desk and wondered what the hell I should be doing.

I expected *assignments*—you know, the editor strolls over and says, "Write this," or "Write that." But as I sat there, I realized I wasn't getting any assignments. You can see my dilemma. I had to write *something*. That's why I was being paid the princely sum of $10 an hour. Sure, I had the police beat (at that time, it entailed driving around to every local city and county station to collect crime reports, accident reports, and so on, and to look for anything that might tangibly make for a good story). But I didn't know what to write about. I went to my editor, who gave me a curious sidelong glance. I asked him what I should write about. He suggested I go over to a local auto parts store because they had just expanded.

So I did.

I wrote 200 words on it. But then I had to write something else.

I contacted an old professor and lamented my cause.

"Frankly, I'm ashamed," he said.

"Why?" I asked, stunned.

"Because you're a reporter. You're supposed to be out enterprise reporting. Did you learn nothing in school?"

Enterprise reporting. Basically it means that you get off your ass, go out, and find a story. Once in a blue moon, good stories fall into your lap while you're sitting at a computer. The rest of the hunt is on you.

So I went out. I saw a sign on the side of a quiet country road on my way to the police station: *WELCOME HOME.* It had military insignias. So I found the family's phone number, and I called them up. What I got from them was an emotional and intense story that appeared in the paper the next day.

And I've been chasing things that could be interesting puddles of words ever since. It's funny: Once you train your mind to be on the hunt for stories, you eventually have many more than you'll ever be able to write. I keep an idea folder in my phone into which I jot everything and anything, and a few persistent nuggets have been in there for years. (Maybe one day I'll have time to write them.)

Coming up with ideas—good ones, sustainable ones, ones readers want and editors salivate over—is no easy task. But it's not the hardest thing in the world, either.

Since you've identified your markets, the next thing to do is get to know them intimately. (That's why it often helps to pitch markets you're already familiar with and read regularly.) Read at least one copy of the latest issue of your target market. If you're really serious, read three.

Then ask yourself: What would readers of this publication want to read? It's time to get those wheels turning. Here are a number of exercises to get you started on your own ideation vacation and generate some solid article ideas.

CHANNEL YOUR EXPERTISE. What knowledge do you possess—or could you find out—that nobody but you could? What do you do in your day job that would fascinate people? What insight into a topic you're obsessed with would a broader audience eat up?

READ LARGE AND THINK SMALL. One easy trick of the trade reporters use is to observe what's in the big national media and then localize it. What national concerns are affecting your own town? Financial crisis was in the national news at one paper I worked for, and we put together a great series on all the abandoned big-box stores in town. Is the keeping of wild pets and the dangers thereof trending in the media? (Did a guy just lose a toe to his pet cheetah?) Find an exotic pet owner or vet in your area, and interview her. The key here is to cover your subject in an honest and organic way that feels fresh—not like you're just riding the coattails of CNN.

THINK SMALL AND PITCH LARGE. Is a big story happening in your neighborhood that a much wider audience would be interested in? Pitch it. It could turn into a news story in a major outlet. Or it could be a narrative feature story in a magazine. There's a lot to be said for the writer who can spot unexplored potential in a simple news story and dig deeper to turn it into a full-fledged narrative. After reading an amazing feature in *Wired* magazine about ten years ago,[1] I e-mailed the writer to ask how the heck she came across such a crazy scoop. Her answer: She saw a blurb about it in her local newspaper and knew there had to be more to the story.

KEEP YOUR EAR TO THE GROUND. Sounds obvious, right? The difference between a writer and a normal person is that a normal person says "Wow" when they hear an amazing story. We say "Wow," too, and then our imaginations get to work figuring out what else there might be to the story—and if it's something worth digging into and sharing with a wider audience. So tune your ear, and always consider what could be a story. This applies to any form of coverage—from a new restaurant coming to town to a career-making news story about a corrupt politician. Talk to people. Building up contacts is key to getting the stories to come to you.

READ INDUSTRY BLOGS AND WEBSITES PERTAINING TO SPECIFIC NICHES. Especially in realms like the science world, there are oodles of sites that publish startling studies that nobody hears about until the right writer at the right general-audience outlet finds them. Do some interviews and broaden the language for a wider readership, and you might have a great piece on your hands.

DON'T SUPPRESS YOUR VOICE. Have a strong opinion about something? Write it down. If it's persuasive enough, there's a good chance it'll see print.

DON'T GET CAUGHT IN THE PAST. Especially for newspapers and weekly markets, don't pitch recaps of past events unless they're still happening when the piece publishes—a concert review or a festival review, for instance. Editors generally don't want them because they look dated and don't serve a reader well. Instead, consider previews. A simple formula I've utilized time and again consists of looking at a calendar of upcoming events, identifying an interesting happening, and then reaching out to the organizer or media contact to find someone with an

---

1 "Flirting with Disaster" by Nadya Labi, about an insane Internet hoax that led to a murder—sort of like the original catfish before the film *Catfish*.

interesting angle or backstory that would make good fodder for a pre-view article of the event. (For example, I wanted to write about an Appalachian festival that was coming to town; the organizer pointed me to a fascinating woman who had been photographing coal miners and whose work was to be featured at the fest.)

BUT DON'T TOTALLY FORGET THE PAST. What are you passionate and knowledgeable about? I've always had a thing for film and theater, and I get a kick out of covering those areas. Events that will be running for a while are entirely fair game to cover—assuming a publication doesn't already have a regular critic assigned to the story. One good strategy is to reach out to the section editor in charge of those areas and offer your services. Should the regular be out of town, you may be on the call list—which means you'll snag the preview tickets to the show.

CONSIDER HOLIDAYS. A cursory glance at the calendar can open up a wealth of ideas. Publications and websites large and small are always seeking timely holiday coverage. Again, the key here is to find a unique way into the topic and to avoid the same old tired story. Rather than simply writing about how a local park is going to have a massive annual holiday light display, why not write about the backbreaking work that goes into setting it up and the stats on the rigs? Rather than writing about how Santa is going to be at the mall, why not interview the Santa, find out who he is as a person and what makes him tick, for a personality profile? I've become addicted to doing this over the years and have interviewed and profiled five or so Santas—all to spectacularly fun (and often spectacularly strange) effect. (As one Santa told me, "The industry gets very competitive. I know other Santas who won't do parties and do exclusive mall work, and some who are pretty pathetic and look like they just need a meal.")

CONSIDER ANNIVERSARIES. Dig into subjects that might have an anniversary year coming up. Your local opera house? A favorite film? There are innumerable ways to cover anniversaries, from retrospectives to the where-are-they-now approach. The history of objects and art pieces merit books of their own because so much blood, sweat, and tears went into them—and many have not been properly documented.

HAUNT THE ARCHIVES. Many museums and city libraries maintain exhaustive local archives that you can check out. Some will require you to break out the microfilm, and others (especially newspaper archives) will often be digitally accessible through the library's website. My advice: Open the archives at random, and see what you find. Remember that "Everybody Has a Story" bit that Steve Hartman used to do on the CBS news, where he'd throw a dart at a map and then go there and pick someone from the phone book to interview? Archives are a lot like that. Dig in, and you'll find a cache of forgotten stories—ones that you can resurrect and follow up on to great effect.

CAPITALIZE ON YOUR STRUGGLES. Brainstorm the hurdles you've recently overcome. Did you just quit smoking in an outside-the-box manner? Did you just successfully overcome installing a new door frame even though you have practically no Mr. Fix-It skills? Did you just get married and pick up some vital tips and tricks of the wedding trade? Don't let your wisdom go to waste. Capitalize on it, and share it with others. Endless publications publish how-tos, from expert business-to-business outlets to consumer magazines and newspapers. (I once wrote a how-to about how to get pulled over, featuring advice from the cops. Unfortunately, I was a staff writer at the time, so it didn't help me pay for the speeding ticket that spurred the idea.)

KEEP AN EYE OUT FOR LOCAL ACCOMPLISHMENTS. Know someone who has published a book, done extraordinary mission work, pulled off an amazing or bizarre feat, or been named to one of those "20 Under 30" lists? That could be a local or national story.

SEEK PASSION. In my experience, passion is at the heart of every good story. Every event, every community happening, every initiative, and every book has a wildly passionate person behind it who went to the often-monumental task of putting it together. Find that person. If you can get him to open up, you just might have a hell of a story on your hands.

CHAPTER 3

THE DREADED PLATFORM DISCUSSION

"I try to make something each year that I can be proud of. If you can do that, year after year, suddenly you've got a career."

—JON WYVILLE

If you've ever tried to publish a book or know someone who has, there's a good chance you've heard that insidious word that strikes fear, dread, and loathing into the heart of many a writer: *platform*. But stay with me, and don't go skipping ahead to the next chapter quite yet: Just because others fear and dread, it doesn't mean you have to. Platform is, basically, the sum total of your network, your visibility, and your reach—in other words, how big your network is, how many copies a publisher thinks you can sell to that network, and what the marketing department of a publisher will inevitably scrutinize when deciding whether or not to green-light your book.[1]

Luckily freelancers don't have to abide by the same rigorous gate-keeping standards novelists and nonfiction book authors do, as our editors won't expect us to sell their magazines for them. But having a simple platform is still important for credibility. If you have a legitimate online presence and some other tricks up your sleeves, you'll be better primed for success.

MAKE YOUR DIGITAL MARK

As an editor, I look for several things beyond the query I receive. The first thing I do: consult Google.

When you Google yourself, what comes up? Do you like it? The results of your search are what your editor will see.

One of my friends, an aspiring filmmaker, once called me with a quandary. He wanted to be known for his film work, but anytime someone Googled him, the first ten hits were all less-than-great blog posts he wrote long ago. He was considering e-mailing the editors of the blogs to ask them to take the posts down or to at least change his name to a pseudonym. Would they care, he wanted to know? Yes, they definitely would care. They would not only be confused but also likely miffed that this person didn't want his name tied to their outlet.

My advice to him: Take control of the digital conversation. Get a website, and post the work you want to be known for. Google is smart (hey, it got rid of content mills, right?), so if you build a website about yourself, in all likelihood, it will turn into the first hit (assuming you don't share a name with a celebrity).

Every freelancer should likewise be taking control of her own platform situation. Think of your website as your online business card—a place where you can share a bio about yourself, samples of your work,

---

[1] How I long for the days of the reclusive genius writer who mails an unmarked package to his publisher, earns a fat check, and sits on the bestseller list for years. Can you imagine the cantankerous fits of rage J.D. Salinger would have displayed if he had to tweet eight times a day about *Catcher in the Rye* or do a book signing at the Mall of America?

and a way to contact you. Simple as that. And don't worry if you don't update it every day: Trust me, most writers' websites are woefully out of date. I try to update mine quarterly, but that often gets pushed to biannually.

If you have modest computer skills, you can build a website yourself on a platform like WordPress, which offers WYSIWYG ("what you see is what you get") design. Granted, what you see is often, um, different from what you get, but with a basic understanding of the platform (you can find thousands of tutorials online) and a little effort on your part, you can use a template and tweak it to look like a professional-grade site.

I created my own site, ZacharyPetit.com, with WordPress. If you want to go the extra mile and avoid the "yourname.wordpress.com" URL and add an additional layer of legitimacy, you can buy your own domain name—"you.com." Sites like GoDaddy.com offer a simple way to do so. On the whole, starting your own website can seem like a daunting task, but it's not that hard once you start digging into it.

GET SOCIAL

For many writers, including me, social media can often make your head feel like it's going to explode. I tend to overthink it. I read too deeply into it. Perhaps it's because we're writers and understand the weight and power of words. (Or at least that's what I tell myself.) When I started my Twitter account, composing a single tweet often caused me twenty minutes of panicked stress; at the time, I didn't fully understand that once I posted it, it probably had five seconds of airtime before it was buried under the greater miasma of tweets on any given user's feed.

But interaction is good. It leads to networking, and to potential assignments.

You may hate to hear this, as I did, but in this day and age, it's a good idea to be on the following sites.

Twitter

Again, Twitter grants visibility and platform. This can be especially important if you do opinion-based writing (in which case you're probably already on Twitter). Follow those you admire, especially fellow writers, editors, and media outlets. You can stay in touch with a publication's stream of activities, and you'll remain in touch with its voice and latest offerings—all things that can help you get to know a market more intimately (which will help you shape your pitches later). As an editor, I've also had writers engage with me on Twitter. When they pitch me later, I know their names and feel more connected, and will respond more personally.

When an editor Googles you and sees that you also have a decent following and are in touch with readers and your craft, it speaks highly to your credibility.

Again, I freely admit that I'm bad at Twitter. But if I were *trying* to be good at Twitter, I'd do the following, which my social media guru colleagues have written about extensively:

- Engage! Spend time interacting with people, and they will follow and interact back.
- Don't follow oodles of people just to get followers; it's better to have more followers than the amount of people you're following.
- Show some personality. Don't fill people's pages with mindless, pointless tweets (save those posts for Facebook).
- Don't just shill your latest article over and over again. Tweet meaningful things and things that others can learn from and/or retweet.
- Don't tweet once upon a blue moon, or you'll basically be me. Nobody wants to follow someone whose last poignant tweet was sent while George W. Bush was in office.

LinkedIn

If your website is your digital business card, then LinkedIn is your digital résumé (literally—that's what it is). It's a good static resource to have on hand for an editor to look at—and, occasionally, people will reach out to you for writing and other gigs. The nice thing about LinkedIn is you can spend as much or as little time on it as you want and have much the same results, unlike Twitter. It can serve as your static résumé, or you can dig into the community elements and converse with publishing and freelance groups, and so on.

BRING IT ON LIKE PATRICK BATEMAN

Okay, this is a bit morbid, but do you remember that brilliant, hilarious, and disturbing scene in *American Psycho* where Patrick Bateman and his colleagues are all showing off their business cards, and Bateman breaks into a cold, jealous sweat over his colleague's off-white, tastefully thick, watermarked business card? That's the reaction you want to evoke.

Well, not really. (And the fact that Bateman loses his mind is probably not something you want to emulate, either.)

In any event, it's always good business to have a business card (especially one that doesn't look like it was printed on industrial toilet paper). You don't have to be employed by a formal institution to have business cards. Any writer, regardless of experience or creds, can create them. Just hop online. I recommend Moo.com, which has a suite of excellently designed templates for writers to choose from. (For the design savvy, you can also create custom cards.)

You can infuse a little personality or flair reflective of your writing style, but it's equally effective to keep it simple and straightforward.

> Zachary Petit
> Freelance Writer
> [phone number]
> [e-mail address]

Distribute early, and distribute often. Because next you'll ...

GET OUT OF THE HOUSE

I know, I know. As writers, we tend to work in solitude, and to be introspective and often a tad camera shy by nature. But not only is getting out and about, and connecting with others a great resource for story ideas, as we discussed earlier, it is also key to building and growing your list of personal contacts, just as you would on Twitter. A massive digital network can amount to beans if you lack a real-world presence.

Attend local writers' nights, community/library gatherings, or meetings for professional writers organizations, such as local Society of Professional Journalists events. You'll meet fellow writers, which is great for both morale and freelance leads. I can't emphasize enough how interconnected publishing is, and how many times a writer friend has said, "You should meet this editor" or "You should pitch that to my editor—I'll connect you two."

And don't miss out on writers conferences. You'll pick up the benefits just mentioned, get great craft instruction, and have a chance to hobnob and connect with the speakers—many of whom are editors. Being able to break the ice in a pitch by saying, "I met you at the Goldmine Freelance Writers Conference in Denver, and you gave me some great advice on …" is a much more effective opening line than the dreaded "Dear Sirs …"

GET GROOMED AND STYLED

Remember how I mentioned that *Writer's Market* is known as the writer's bible? Well, the *Associated Press Stylebook* is known as the journalist's bible. Pick up a copy to peruse, and begin to familiarize yourself with all the useful information it contains. Essentially, it dictates how to format your articles, how to punctuate properly, and on and on. In publishing, the hierarchy for how an editor makes style decisions is generally as follows.

- **HOUSE STYLE.** Most publications abide by their own house styles. House styles spell out all sorts of weird rules and absurdly nitpicky things, like how to format the word *bestseller*, or whether the names of movies should be in quotes or italicized. Luckily, writers generally don't have to concern themselves with house styles, as they are so varied and random. (But if you begin to regularly write for a publication, it's good form to request a copy of the house style and study it.) For anything that isn't in a publication's house style, they defer to …

- **THE ASSOCIATED PRESS STYLEBOOK**. Available in print form, as an online subscription (which I like for its easy searchability), and as an app for nerds on the go, AP Style covers the usage rules for an enormous amount of basic terms and amazingly precise, if not obscure, ones. (Who knew that a *lectern* is something one stands behind and a *podium* is something one stands *on top of*? Get it right or the AP will smack you with a ruler.) Anything not included in AP Style defers to …

- **WEBSTER'S NEW WORLD COLLEGE DICTIONARY (FOURTH EDITION).** Wish I was joking, but this tome really has been perched atop my desk for years. The NWCD catchall has luckily (and finally) been incorporated into AP's online stylebook, meaning we no longer have to constantly thumb through the print edition.

You may be wondering: Why do editors care about all this crap? The short answer: Following a usage guide breeds consistency in every single issue. And consistency is professionalism and quality (and a nervous breakdown about Massachusetts versus Mass. versus MA averted).

As a writer, what does this mean to you? Basically, a good working knowledge of AP Style will let an editor know that you're capable and detail oriented. And that's worth its weight in gold, especially with so many writers pitching editors from every angle every moment of the day. And here's a tip: Writing your query in AP Style will win you bonus points.

BUILD UP YOUR CALLUSES

In 1961, before she'd stopped talking to us press hounds, Harper Lee was asked by *Writer's Digest* for her single best piece of writing advice.[2] Her response: "I would advise anyone who aspires to a writing career that before developing his talent he would be wise to develop a thick hide." It stands true today, if not more so now than ever, with the anonymous open forum that the Internet provides. People can be downright demonic with their comments. Take criticism where it holds true. Learn from it. As for the trolls who troll for the sheer sociopathic joy of tearing

---

2 In the piece, WD also referred to her as the author of *To Kill a Hummingbird*. Maybe that's why she stopped talking to the press.

something down and watching someone squirm, that's what trolls do: They troll (on Amazon, Goodreads, Twitter, etc.). As I've said before, it's not personal. Which means the message at the core of their words means as little as the 0s and 1s used to code it. Ignore them heartily.

In your career, you'll face a rainbow of opinions, both positive and negative. You'll learn to love the positive and become enraged by the negative—but only for your allotted five minutes, okay? Then it's time to move on and keep writing, trolls be damned.

PRACTICE THE ART OF THE LITERARY THANK YOU NOTE

Here's where I begin to get a bit esoteric. Years ago, I commissioned the author Sherman Alexie to write a piece about the "Top 10 Pieces of Writing Advice" he'd been given (which he subsequently retitled "The Top 10 Pieces of Writing Advice I've Been Given … Or That I'll Pretend Were Given to Me). His No. 1 nugget of advice: "When you read a piece of writing that you admire, send a note of thanks to the author. Be effusive with your praise. Writing is a lonely business. Do your best to make it a little less lonely." That one has stuck with me. I tend to do it not only for books I read and admire, but also for magazine articles that blow me away. I'm never seeking anything in return. I just want the writer to know that what she spent so much time on—so much literary blood, sweat, and tears—was worth it and truly resonated with someone. Call it karmic. Call it paying it forward. Call it the writerly circle of life. Whenever anyone sends me such a note, it never fails to make my day—and I keep a folder of these notes for the bad days (especially when those trolls come out of their caves). I'd recommend doing the same.

CHAPTER 4

FINDING A WAY IN

"Write. Rewrite. When not writing or rewriting, read. I know of no shortcuts."
—LARRY L. KING

"Interesting things happen when the creative impulse is cultivated with curiosity, freedom, and intensity."
—SAUL BASS

"Long patience and application saturated with your heart's blood—you will either write or you will not—and the only way to find out whether you will or not is to try."
—JIM TULLY

Before I start rambling about queries and pitching (and believe me, there will be rambling, given the vital nature of the subject), let's first talk about the different types of pieces you can pitch.

The first big question: Do you like to write short, or do you like to write long?

I love both. They're each imbued with their share of writerly challenges, and neither is a simple walk in the park. I naturally write long, which has its perks when I'm striving to fill newspaper pages. But I'm sure I've given some editors a brief panic attack by blowing a word count by 1,000 or more words.[1]

This may come as a surprise, but of anything I write, the hardest by far is the content I pen for *National Geographic Kids*—especially when it's something like a one-page column that runs at 300 words. Not only is writing for kids extraordinarily difficult—especially as it pertains to word choice, utilizing references kids today can understand, and the like—but since it's *National Geographic*, I'm often dealing with advanced, specialized, scientific topics, and must distill them for the appropriate audience. I spend as much time penning a 6,000-word feature story for an adult magazine as I do an 800-word kid's story. Writing short is all about writing tight—cutting all the fat until only the most essential elements remain (which, for the record, you should also do for longer pieces). Writing short, especially for NGK, has undoubtedly made me a better writer.

On the flip side, many see writing long as the bigger challenge. Word counts can seem daunting. It can be hard to maintain a consistent voice and tone throughout a piece, or to give a long story a narrative arc, or to make the piece read as a cohesive whole.

Regardless of whether you prefer longer or shorter, many opportunities for both await in magazines and other media. Using an issue

---

1 Since this is an instructional book about freelance writing, it's my duty to advise that you *never* do this. Giving your editors brief panic attacks is not a good idea. Always give your editors what they ask for. *However*, I should add that if you write for me, or others like me, I'll probably let you write as long as you want, within reason. When dealing with highly specialized content, be it about design or the craft of writing, as an editor, I like to have the option to trim certain things that I know our audience is already aware of, that we covered last issue, or that have been covered elsewhere in the feature package, etc.

of *Writer's Digest* as an example, let's flip through the types of articles available (and unavailable) to freelancers and break down an entire magazine to give a deeper insight into how everything works. Though publications all have individual collections of stories, most follow a variant of the same basic approach or piece these sections together in different ways to create their own puzzle. For now, don't worry about the actual writing formula for these pieces—we'll get into that later.

A GUIDED TOUR OF A MAGAZINE

COVER

Every magazine has their own cover procedure—and, often, their own *formula*. At WD, the author featured in the big Q&A within graces the cover 99 percent of the time. WD's designer works with the graphic elements, and the editor drafts the coverlines. They are then sent to the publisher for approval. At *Print*, the art director works with an outside illustrator or creates the cover imagery himself. We brainstorm the coverlines as a staff, and then I make final selections and sharpen them. The publisher and circulation specialists then review the final package.

WRITING OPPORTUNITY: No, obviously. But it's kind of interesting nonetheless, right?

TABLE OF CONTENTS/EDITOR'S LETTER/MASTHEAD

These sections are the purview of the editorial team. However, some magazines do have small pieces or interesting factoids that some freelancer or another pens.

WRITING OPPORTUNITY: Generally, no.

READER MAIL

You're likely familiar with this general mailbag section. I'm often asked whether you can use letters to the editor as writing samples. Unfortunately, while it's always a cool honor to have your letter run in a magazine and have your voice heard, letters don't carry weight among editors.

"'Get in Good With Goodreads' was clear and concise and I immediately understood how this would benefit my career as a writer."

FINDING A NEW PLATFORM

February's issue was one of the best you have done. I had heard of Goodreads but figured it was just another Facebook and not worth my time. Michael J. Sullivan's article, "Get in Good With Goodreads," was clear and concise and I immediately understood how this would benefit my career as a writer. My account is now set up!

Thank you for the great magazine. I always learn something new.

Warren W. Nast
Camp Hill, Pa.

WRITING OPPORTUNITY: No. But technically, yes.

THE FRONT OF THE BOOK

Now, finally, we hit the sweet spot! At WD, the first chunk of the magazine preceding the longer feature articles is called "Inkwell." Fronts of the book (bewildering editor-speak for everything in the front of the *magazine*) are gold mines for breaking in. At many publications, this is the best place to get a foot in the door. As editor of this section, I would comb the general submissions in-box for pieces to run every issue. If the submissions in-box didn't have something specific I was looking for, I'd reach out to a trusted writer (often the people whose work I had picked out of the submissions in-box and run previously) to see if they had an interest in working on a piece I was seeking. Front-of-the-book articles run the gamut, from 800-word general articles to opinion pieces to infographics to short Q&As to reviews of anything and everything to poppy 100-word content often referred to (and maligned!) as "filler" (hey, someone gets paid for those factoids, right?). Most front-of-the-book sections follow a formula. As such, if you can decipher that formula by looking through some back issues, you can figure out exactly what the magazine is looking for, and know what to pitch.

When I was at WD, the formula for the front of the book was:

1. An 800-word lede[2] article.
2. A backup lede article of roughly the same length.
3. Robert Lee Brewer's poetry column.
4. The Good to Know column—this piece explains in practical terms the differences in things that are similar but not the same (think the difference between revolvers and semiautomatic pistols, or between a psychologist and a psychiatrist) that all writers should know for either their fiction or nonfiction.
5. One-page random article, if space allows, occasionally a Q&A.
6. 5-Minute Memoir (see next paragraph).

The beauty of front-of-the-book sections is that they give an editor a low-risk way to try out a writer. (If a short piece doesn't work, the editor can quickly replace it with something else she has on tap or waiting in the wings.) Thus, if you're trying to break in, you have a greater chance in this section than in the feature well, where you'd be compet-

---

2 Delightfully misspelled journalistic jargon for an opening piece or opening line.

ing with the magazine's trusted regular writers. Once you've broken in, you can naturally work your way up to those feature articles.

WRITING OPPORTUNITY: Yes! Times one thousand.

THE ESSAY SECTION

WD's essay section is called 5-Minute Memoir (and it is exactly that— a short narrative essay from a writer reflecting on some element of the craft or the lifestyle, with a nugget of wisdom takeaway). You'll find great essay sections in publications small and large, ranging from insanely short to insanely long, and they're perfect places to get your foot in the door. Bonus: Generally, editors don't require you to have any published clips under your belt in order to write one of these. (See the "How High?" section later in this chapter.)

WRITING OPPORTUNITY: Yes! Times 1,001.

THE FEATURE WELL

The feature well is where the magic happens in magazines. Editors often approach the well in two ways when planning an issue: They either curate a "themed" issue, with a collection of articles centered around the same topic, or they acquire a hodgepodge of feature arti-cles that aren't necessarily connected but are loyal to the magazine's mission statement and readership. (In the latter approach, the most appealing core feature will then be selected to hold the greatest visual weight on the cover.)

Feature stories are wide ranging and often take the following forms:

- **JOURNALISTIC FEATURES:** An article that tells a story, be it news related or human-interest related, through interviews with multiple sources and exposition from the author.
- **Q&A INTERVIEWS:** Generally reserved for the rich and famous subjects that readers want direct insight (or answers) from. One note: In general, the magazine's in-house team or most trusted freelancers handle pieces dealing with celebrities. Unless you have a direct "in" with a person, it can be futile to pitch a publication a piece on a celebrity to whom you don't already have access.
- **THE PROFILE** (also adorably referred to in Journalism 101 class-es as "The Personality Profile"): This is, by far, my favorite type of piece to write. It's a cousin of the Q&A, but it tends to go much deeper: It involves the writer's insights and take on the subject, versus just the subject's words, and employs a strong narrative el-ement. Subjects can be anyone from a celebrity to a garbage man. It can tightly focus on the subject or involve the voices of multiple sources. Always a true challenge to write, and always a worthy (and incredibly fun) one. In my opinion, *Esquire*'s Tom Chiarella is the best profile writer on the planet. If you want to learn how to write brilliant profiles, read his work. It's no small feat to cover the celebrities he covers—who have all been written about god knows how many times by others—and still make the story fresh, relevant, and wildly readable.
- **THE HOW-TO:** Simple and straightforward enough, as discussed earlier. For publications that specialize in how-to content, like *Writer's Digest*, these pieces are generally penned by experts. But that's not the case in every publication. Many will take articles based on

fresh advice from a variety of writers, especially if they've just successfully accomplished what they're proposing a how-to on. How-tos can either be written in a third-person or first-person perspective.

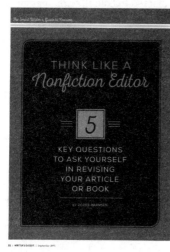

WRITING OPPORTUNITY: High. The odds are ever in your favor the more experience you have.

THE BACK OF THE BOOK

Some magazines have one, some magazines don't. Think front of the book, but in the, uh, back. Often consists of a repository of stray or recurring columns, reviews, and similar content.

STANDOUT**MARKETS**

CONFERENCE**SCENE**

WRITING OPPORTUNITY: Indeed.

THE BACK PAGE

Back pages are a reader (and editor) favorite. They may take the form of essays, previews to the next issue (boooooring), and, often, humor. *Esquire* and *Wired* have great humor back pages that ring true to their audience and style. The back page of *Print* is one of my favorite sections—"The Last Word" is an illustrated take on a famous person's dying words (sounds morbid, but it's actually delightful and often funny). *Writer's Digest* publishes "Reject a Hit"—a fake rejection letter to a famous book that often mocks foolhardy editors who either misunderstood the work or have god-awful judgment. I wrote the first installment a while back, but freelance writers have since taken up the duty (and to greater effect), and anyone with the ability to condense their wit into 300 words can write for the section. It's basically writer porn. The moral of the story: Study back pages. Again, it doesn't matter how much experience you have, so long as you can write something hilarious that's a great fit for the section.

WRITING OPPORTUNITY: Git 'er done.

THE BRAVE NEW WORLD OF BREAKING IN

Everyone wants a slot in the print issue, right? (I do.) Well, sometimes the best way to get your foot in the door is through a publication's Web counterpart. Websites need fresh content. Always. And though editors all publish their print articles on their websites as well, they also want Web exclusives so they're not just rehashing content online. For the website, they need to generate a stream of fresh output, to maintain a conversation with their readers, to fit the paradigm of shorter Web content versus their long-form reads, to fill their newsletters with fresh content, and also to satisfy the SEO gods who tend to run their businesses.

The upside: It's not all that difficult to break into many outlets, and once you've done so, you'll have a contact in the building and can build up both a relationship with your editor and opportunities for expansion. The downside: More often than not the pay for online work will be laughably bad (assuming there is pay). But if you can get a clip from a major outlet's Web presence, in my opinion, it's worth it. The Huffington Post is a bad example because they don't publish a print edition, but remember: They pay no one. But a byline from The Huffington Post? I'd take it. A friend of mine recently broke into *Sports Illustrated* online. I don't know if he got paid, but I was still envious. When *McSweeney's* published a piece of mine, my inner joy in the long run far outweighed whatever dinner I could have bought with the proceeds.

As McSweeney's Internet Tendency says in their submission guidelines, "PAYMENT: There will likely be none. If there is any, it may come very late or in unusual currency."

HOW HIGH?

Now let's take a moment to discuss a potential game changer in your career.

Common journalistic wisdom has always held that you need to start all the way at the bottom of the sea floor, and you can then work your way up to the gratifying oxygen gulp that is a major publication. It's sound advice—and logical advice, when you consider how many people have gotten their start that way—but it's not the only advice.

Want to write for *The New York Times*? Well, try it.

Allow me to explain. When I started at *Writer's Digest*, I was put in charge of the Nonfiction column, which at the time was written by a brilliant, charming, hilarious Manhattan writer named Susan Shapiro.

In one of the columns I edited, she suggested going straight for the top and writing for the big boys and girls right out of the gate. I'm a journalist by nature, meaning I'm overly skeptical and a tad surly about most things.[3]

Bullshit, I first thought.

---

3 To the endless irritation of my wife. But she's a journalist, too. So I'm just going to tell myself that she's being skeptical and surly of my skepticism and surliness, because it's what she's programmed to do, and that it's no fault of my character.

But over the years, *I saw it work.* Susan teaches a class titled "Instant Gratification Takes Too Long," which, again, may sound like snake oil for writers who should instead be toiling away for thirty years at a newspaper before attempting to pitch the big guns. But then you look at her students, all previously unpublished writers, and you see their first bylines in *The New York Times,* an assortment of major women's magazines, and many other outlets.

She and her students are proof that you don't necessarily have to start at the bottom. If you shoot for the top and you've got the chops, you might get there. Obviously, landing your first clip in general is a gratifying and thrilling prospect no matter where it is. But it doesn't hurt to have a powerhouse under your belt.

So how do you do it? In my opinion,[4] it depends on *what* you write. The chances of having no clips or reporting experience and landing an investigative journalistic feature in *Wired* magazine are nil. Editors need to know and feel confident that you can do what you're proposing to do for such a piece, and seeing previous examples of that work helps them sleep better at night. Moreover, the highest echelon of publications, like, say, *The New Yorker,* has thousands of writers querying it at any one time, and competition is hilariously fierce. Once, at *The New Yorker*'s office high in the Manhattan clouds, I asked the features editor what it takes to break into the magazine with a feature article. His advice: Wait—years, if need be—until you have that *one* perfect, refined idea that you feel truly merits the scale and readership of the publication. Now, that may sound like the sort of arrogant counsel you'd expect from *The New Yorker,* but it's true. You've got to present your very best to such publications, and you've got to have an idea that will blow them out of the water. Otherwise you're wasting their time and, moreover, yours. (For the record, I'm still ~~trying~~ waiting to come up with that pitch.)

Again, breaking into the top when you're all the way at the bottom depends on *what* you write. A big journalistic feature? Not likely. But if you can pen a shorter piece *ahead* of time and submit it to an editor

---

4 And I suppose you'll know whether Susan agrees, should she decide to blurb this book. Trial by fire!

complete, rather than pitching it, then you've gained a rare advantage: Your writing can speak for itself.[5]

Essay sections—which, as mentioned earlier, an overwhelming amount of magazines, online outlets, major newspapers, and so on publish—can be a great way to break into the big leagues. Write a great essay, and an editor will publish it. Simple as that. She doesn't care in the least if you haven't been published anywhere else first. She wants a fresh voice and a good piece. At *Writer's Digest,* I published dozens of essays from people no one had heard of but who could write their faces off.

Susan is a big advocate of what she calls "The Humiliation Essay"—in which a writer reveals all and channels his most embarrassing story for readers in print.[6] And, as I've seen many times now, it works. Match your essay idea to a fitting section in a publication, and you've got a good recipe on your hands.

When it comes to that first clip: If you've got something good, go big (meaning send it to your favorite powerhouse publication). If it doesn't hit, work your way down the list, get it published, and then work your way back up with your next articles.

---

[5] This is called on-spec writing and is admittedly a controversial subject. More on that later.

[6] Susan wrote a piece on this for me. Check out "No Reservations" at writersdigest.com/essential-guide-to-freelance-writing.

CHAPTER 5

PITCH PERFECT

"Don't worry about people stealing your ideas. If your ideas are any good, you'll have to ram them down people's throats."
—HOWARD H. AIKEN

"If you're not pitching, stop bitching"
—REBECCA AGUILAR

"Walk on air against your better judgment."
—SEAMUS HEANEY

The workshop I present most frequently at writers conferences is called "The Good, the Bad, and the Nightmare Query." It usually begins with the following story—my own personal nightmare query experience. You'd be surprised how many editors have one (or several) of these under their belts.

Very early in my career, fueled by a steady stream of Hunter S. Thompson books and freelance writing ignorance, I had an idea: I wanted to write an epic review of a Jackie Chan movie called *The Tuxedo*. Anyone remember it? Essentially it was about a bumbling fool who found a magical tuxedo that gave him all sorts of superspy powers.

Sounds terrible, right?

That's what I thought, too—and what I was hoping for.

I had a press pass to go see it, so I saw it—and, yes, in my opinion, it was indeed terrible. Laughably bad. Which was great news for the piece I wanted to write. The resulting article was a sprawling 2,000-word magnum opus movie review in the form of an apology from Jackie Chan to moviegoers. I thought it was brilliant. So I sent it off to an editor I knew, and now refuse to name out of humiliation, and sat around waiting for my check, affirmation of my hilarity, and some complimentary copies to frame around my apartment.

Eventually the editor sent me a response. And in three words, he taught me the most valuable lesson of querying freelance articles in one fell swoop:

What the hell?

We'll get back to that in just a moment.

When I started maintaining submissions in-boxes and accepting/rejecting freelance queries, my writing world changed. It was eye-opening. It was mind-blowing, in both good and bad ways. And doing it for years has taught me a hell of a lot about shaping my own queries. Unlike a lot of things in the writing world, queries are generally not subjective. There are objectively great queries, and there are objectively awful queries. I want to share with you a medley of both so that you can apply those lessons to your own writing, and make sure you wind up with more of the former and less of the latter.

At *Writer's Digest*, I'd go through the hundreds of submissions every Friday. I'd save the good ones for follow-up on Monday. If you ever got a response from the WD submissions in-box on a Friday, it probably wasn't good news.[1]

So let's make sure that every day is a Monday. (Wait, that came out wrong. That would be terrible. But you know what I mean.) This is a chapter of Dostoyevsky-like proportions—and for good reason. Querying is one of the most vital things in all of freelance writing.

So let's journey onward, comrades.[2]

THE NIGHTMARE QUERY

If we start at the bottom of the barrel, the worst of the worst, we can only go up, right? The good queries featured here are all 100-percent untouched. The bad queries you're about to read are all based on real queries—names and identifying characteristics have been changed to protect the identities of those included.[3]

Now, before we start, a word about the bad queries and why I'm including them here. I'm not doing it to shame the original responsible parties or to make you laugh (though some can be pretty funny, right?). Rather, I believe that bad queries contain as many lessons as good queries do—and understanding both will make you a better querier. If you can see how and why something went wrong, you can avoid doing that thing yourself. Seeing a medley of great queries all in one spot is nice, but it's only half the coin.

So, to start, have a look at this.

> DEAR SIRS
> ID LIKE YOU TO PUBLISH MY WIFE'S POETRY. IT'S NOT VERY GOOD. BUT ITS OK. WILL YOU DO THAT?
>   PLEASE LET ME KNOW.

Yes! That was an actual query—an honest-to-god real-world submission to a real magazine.

---

1 Having to reject articles at a magazine that advocates for writers makes you feel like a total asshole. What's worse: People pitch a lot of stories about rejection. Rejecting an article about rejection? It's both ironic and heartbreaking, and I await the karma police.

2 For more query letter examples, turn to the Appendix.

3 And to protect myself from being sued.

Aside from writing this query in all caps—WHICH YOU SHOULD NEVER DO—the first obvious mistake is the greeting. "Dear Sirs"—or, rather, "DEAR SIRS"—not only showcases a comically outdated mindset (throughout my career, the majority of editors I have worked for have been women), but it also displays a stunning lack of research. It's not hard to pick up a copy of a magazine you want to write for and to find the appropriate editor's name and presumed gender (more on that in just a moment).

If a writer can't be bothered to do even the most basic level of research, how can an editor trust him to write a detail-driven piece?

But, most important, this query calls into play the most essential lesson of querying magazines and publications—I am referring to what the "What the hell?" response I received for my Jackie Chan epic taught me. The lesson is this: *Before you ever send a query for anything, read the publication you're querying first.*

Moreover, read two to three back issues to really get a good feel for the outlet.

Now, this may seem overly obvious and might make you want to fling this book across the room, but hear me out. There's a deeper level to it, and it can indeed be a tall order. When you're a freelancer—and especially if you're a pro freelancer—you must send out dozens of queries on a constant basis in order to land assignments and keep bread on the table. It may seem like an insurmountable task to read every publication you're pitching—but it's essential that you do. (Someone recently countered my point by saying, "Why? If I want to write for *Dog Fancy*, I'll just send them a story about my dog!" I responded by informing him that *Dog Fancy* no longer exists.)

In the case of the good husband/poetry enthusiast who penned the all-caps query, if this gentleman had actually ever read *Writer's Digest*, he would have known it was a how-to magazine. It doesn't publish unsolicited poetry, short stories, fiction, or anything along those lines, as a literary journal would.

On the same token, had I actually read the publication I was pitching with my Jackie Chan review, I would have known that their movie reviews tended to be 200-word recaps of films, with a standard thumbs up or down. In other words, not the best venue for a 2,000-word (brilliant) screed written in the voice of Jackie Chan.

As I mentioned earlier, you must know your markets so you don't waste an editor's time—and, more important, your own.

GONE TO MARKET

So now we return to the market discussion. Once you know whom you want to write for, always read that publication's submission guidelines before you do anything else. Even if you're the laziest scribe on earth, which I am at times, all you have to do is Google the magazine's name plus "Submission Guidelines," and more often than not, you'll get it straight from the horse's mouth (the publication's website) or from one of the many aggregators of such information on the Web.

Once you have those submission guidelines, you must follow them to a T. Some publications are more particular about this than others. As you can probably guess, I (and many others like me) couldn't care less how the thing is formatted, so long as it contains a great idea. But it's always best to play it safe, so do what the guidelines say, and play by their rules.

The guidelines will tell you who to query. (No more "Dear Sirs.") They'll tell you when to query. They'll tell you how to query. They'll tell you what types of pieces the publication buys from freelancers. They'll tell you what types of pieces the publication doesn't buy. They'll probably include oddly specific rules that seem to make no sense and are the purview of an obsessive-compulsive editor who combs his hair exactly forty-two times every morning and throws a hissy fit if the ratio of his imported coffee to soy milk is the slightest bit off. But haters gonna hate, and gatekeepers gonna gate.[4]

If a publication says not to include attachments, don't include attachments.[5]

---

4 With further apologies to my editor. I CAN'T STOP DOING IT.

5 This, at least, goes beyond nitpicky and is someone else's call. Our IT departments break out in cold sweats at the thought of anonymous people sending us foolhardy, non-tech-savvy editors random files laden with a whole Petri dish full of computer viruses. As editors, we fear opening these attachments and suffering the wrath of an IT worker gone postal. IT guys seem gentle and nice enough, but they're much like cats: cute until the claws come out and better left to daydream by the heater.

If the submission guidelines say to submit only via e-mail, don't send a massive package through the postal service. It will likely, to the detriment of both the writer and Mother Earth, be thrown out.

If a publication says to submit your query in Comic Sans, 10.5 font, with 1.5" margins, red text, and a blue background, indulge them.

Why all these silly rules? Nitpicking. But consider that most "slush piles"—the name for the general in-box that all these random queries wind up in—stretch into the hundreds, if not thousands. When an editor is desperately trying to get through all of these queries before the clock hits 5 P.M. (or, more typically, 10 P.M.), it's logical that they're looking for any reason to discount a submission and thin the herd. Editors want good queries. They *love* good queries. But more often than not, the ones that don't follow the most basic rules are the ones that aren't any good.

So don't give an editor an excuse to be an asshole and throw the baby out with the bathwater. Get your good writing read. Follow the rules.

As I said before, books like *Writer's Market* and their online equivalents are gold mines for such resources and will give you everything you need in one place, potentially saving valuable time that you can then spend writing.

PROCESS DOCS

Before we review some actual queries (and reveal my secret strategy for query success), let me address something I always wondered about until I found myself in the thick of the publishing business: *How does the editorial process work—how does an editor assess queries?*

All publications handle it differently (especially varying based on their size), but here's an example of how things have been done at three of my magazines.

First, the editor sets herself up on an IKEA throne, and, then after being fed quinoa and organic truffles by an intern, she opens her browser and braces herself for the medley of rough decisions to come.

At *Writer's Digest*, the managing editor is usually responsible for going through the slush pile (and keeping it from becoming too unwieldy and too out of date). I'd start at the top of the in-box (the most recent queries) and quickly look through the new submissions to make sure we wouldn't miss out on any time-sensitive queries. For instance, something like: "Stephen King is coming over to my house today, and today only. Can I interview him for you?" In which case, the answer would be yes.

After making sure Stephen King wasn't headed over to anyone's house that particular day, I'd scroll all the way down to the bottom of the in-box—first come, first served. Our submissions response time was stated at two to four months. Sometimes writers would get a response in a few hours, and sometimes it would take the full four months (or, admittedly, longer), depending on where we were in the production cycle. That's the tricky thing about submissions: As an editor, they're tough to manage—especially if you get a lot of submissions and have a small staff. (Trust me, all of us wish we had the luxury of having a dedicated acquisitions editor.) I'm not making excuses,[6] but when you're an editor and have to follow up with ten writers before noon about stories in progress, lay out a storyboard for the next issue, copyedit five features, and write a couple of magazine columns and blog posts before the day is up, the submissions in-box often falls to the bottom of the priority list.

All of this is to say: If you don't hear back right away, don't take it personally. It's not a reflection of your query at all but rather the editor's questionably large schedule. (In a moment I'll share with you a great way to get faster responses.)

The good thing is that the editor *will* get to that submissions in-box. She needs content to put in her issues, and the submissions in-box is a one-stop shop for ideas catering directly to her publication.

So I'd work my way up from the oldest queries to the new ones. If something looked promising for a feature, I'd send it to the editor in chief for consideration. If it looked good for a front-of-the-book piece or another section I oversaw, I'd reach out to the writer directly. If it seemed like a match for one of our columns, I'd send it to that column's appropriate editor. The editor would then respond with a yes, a no, or a request for more info, and we'd go from there.

Any query that didn't seem like a good match for the magazine would get a form rejection letter slightly modified to fit what the writer

---

6 Okay, maybe I am. But still.

had submitted. (This is something else we hate doing—but it must be done to conserve time, so we can move on to the next query, and more important, keep making magazines.)

At *Print* and *HOW* magazines, we follow the same basic approach, but an associate editor goes through the submissions. The top editors often end up making assignments by reaching out to a trusted pool of contributors for article ideas and pitches every issue, or by fielding queries that come directly to their personal in-boxes.

Which brings me to my next big point …

YOU SHOULD AVOID THE SLUSH PILE ENTIRELY

In the preceding pages, you've probably come to a realization: The slush pile is a pretty damn terrible place to be. Form letters can be demeaning (especially when an editor has weird formatting issues).[7] Queries can languish for months (unless Stephen King is coming over for dinner). And as someone who has received a rejection letter to something I submitted a year earlier and actually *forgot* about, rest assured that makes it twice as painful.

So why should you keep submitting to slush piles?

You shouldn't.

As both a writer and an editor, I can tell you that reaching out directly to an editor and thereby skipping the slush, is a far more effective strategy. I started doing this in my freelance work because so many writers were successfully doing it to me as an editor.

As I said earlier, dedicated acquisitions editors have gone the way of the dodo at most publications. So let's decipher the Morse code of a theoretical masthead so you understand the responsibilities of various staff members and can determine who to send your query to. The tricky

---

7 Which leads to a ridiculous response that looks like this:

Dear **Zachary**

We regret to inform you that your submission **"How to Write an Article About How to Write a Book on Freelancing"** was not a good fit for our publication. Thanks for sending it, though.

Editor

thing is that the following terms have different definitions depending on the publication—but for the most part, this is the general hierarchy:

PUBLISHER

Caters to the business side of things and the execs. Often feared by editorial staffers.

EDITOR IN CHIEF

The top dog, editorially speaking. Sets overall content strategy, writes eloquent editor's letters. Makes appearances. Sometimes writes features. At smaller publications, they're more hands-on with articles.

EXECUTIVE EDITOR

One rung below the editor in chief. Often tends to more day-to-day matters.

MANAGING EDITOR

At some publications, they're editorially hands-on and may edit, write, look at queries, etc.; at others, they focus more on managing staff and overseeing production schedules.

SENIOR EDITOR

A high-level employee who often edits and writes. More likely to handle more robust content, such as feature articles.

ASSOCIATE EDITOR

A step above an assistant editor. May write, edit, or do clerical work. More likely to handle front-of-the-book content and columns.

ASSISTANT EDITOR

One step below an associate editor. May write, edit, or do clerical work. More likely to handle front-of-the-book content.

COPYEDITOR

Responsible for catching errors and style inconsistencies that the editors miss.

RESEARCH ASSISTANT (AND SIMILAR TITLES FOUND IN MASTHEADS)

A luxury staffer smaller publications wish they had.

PITCH PERFECT

INTERN
Beacon of light.

CONTRIBUTING EDITORS/EDITORS AT LARGE

Ever wonder what these people do? This is where things can get confusing, and where different publications tend to branch off into their own creative terminology. Often these are just creatives with whom the publication works on a regular basis and who deserve recognition for that. *Print* magazine's contributing editor Steven Heller, for example, has been writing for the magazine for thirty years. Contributing editors are not in-house, and they're not full-time employees.[8] Oh, and generally, they don't edit anything; they just write. Makes sense, right? No. No, it does not.

So that's your lineup of the usual suspects. Which one is going to be lucky enough to get your query? If a publication doesn't have an acquisitions editor and no one specific is listed in the submissions guidelines, again, don't resort to the slush pile. My advice: Send it to the managing editor. That's your sweet spot.

Why the M.E.? Most managing editors serve as a critical cog in the wheel of a publication. They may be responsible for combing through queries, but even if they're not, they know who should get your query and can forward it to the right editor to get you a response.

When it comes to tracking down an editor's direct e-mail address, it's not all that difficult to unearth. First, check the "Contact Us" section on the publication's website. Sometimes you get lucky and each staffer is listed with their corresponding e-mail address. If not, fear not—you'll be able to find it elsewhere on the Web.

It used to be that you could Google "zacharypetit@" and stumble upon an e-mail address. But nowadays, that'll only bring up my woefully unupdated Twitter account because Twitter stole @ from the rest of us.

Here's how the modern freelance sleuth works. Let's say you were trying to find my e-mail address. It's not on a "Contact Us" website. It's not in a market book listing for *Print* magazine, because we put

---

8 Supposedly the phrasing "editor at large" comes from *High Times* magazine's heyday in the 1970s (back when it was a journalistic enterprise and not a how-to for growing weed) and referred to a certain editor who was constantly MIA in the office.

our slush pile address there. So you'd head over to *Print*'s website and try to find *any* e-mail address. By poking around you'd easily turn up the slush pile address, printmag@fwmedia.com. (F+W is the owner of *Print*.) That gives you the first crucial part: fwmedia.com. That's half your puzzle right there. Next, you would want to figure out the naming convention. By digging around some more, you could easily turn up the name of a PR person for F+W or a customer service rep—**jane. smith**@fwmedia.com. That gives you the rest of the formula: first name [dot] last name. From there, you can deduce that my e-mail address is zachary.petit@fwmedia.com.

But how can you trust it? Google it: "zachary.petit@fwmedia.com" (quotes and all). My e-mail address pops up from various aggregators and directories, and maybe a press release or two I've written.

Once you're confident you have the right address, send your query off. If it bounces, you'll know you've done something wrong. If it doesn't, you can assume you did something right.

Sending directly to the right editor will do two critical things:

1. Your query will be read exponentially faster. Simply put, on a psychological level, if a query is addressed to the correct editor with her correct name, correctly spelled and lacking all trappings of "DEAR SIRS," the editor will have a more personal connection to the query—and thus a greater liability. Queries with my name on them get a response, if only because I look like a jerk if I don't reply. Simple—and effective—psychology. It's a lot easier for an institution to ignore a random query addressed to no one than it is a query calling someone to the floor and personally inviting her to check something out.

2. Even more important, addressing your query to the right person shows editors that you're a real player in the game: *that you know what you're doing.* And believe me, that's vital. Slush piles tend to be filled with queries that are overwhelmingly bad. If you submit to a slush pile, your query is going to be surrounded top to bottom

by queries for poetry that we don't publish, penis enlargement ads, offers for luxury charter airplanes,[9] and a sea of queries that just aren't good fits. Editors are trained to expect the worst. If you can do this one simple thing, you automatically show the editor that you know how to play the game, which gives him a greater degree of confidence in reading your query. The next step is to nail the rest of the query. If you can do that, you'll get an assignment.

A word to the wise, though: Only go so far in contacting editors directly. The surest way to ruin a grumpy editor's day is to *call* him with a query. Never, ever cold call an editor unless you already have a relationship with him. I've spent many an afternoon squirming on the other end of a phone while a writer walks me through her story, step by step, over the course of forty-five minutes as I desperately attempt to interject so I can explain that we don't accept queries over the phone and ask her to e-mail me the idea so I can give it a deeper look.

The good news is that even if an editor is a black hole on the Internet and his contact info is nowhere to be found, you still have options. In the subject line to your slush pile query, address it as follows:

ATTN: Zachary Petit. 10 Things Every Creative Should Know

By doing that, you're already rising to the top, and I'm going to click on it. If an associate editor is sorting through the slush, she knows to forward it to me.

Standing out from the pack—especially when most of the pack isn't trying to stand out—isn't hard.

THE GOAL

In a query, you're trying to explain to an editor why she should pay to play or why she should request your full manuscript.

Seems rather convoluted, doesn't it? Let me explain.

---

9 Really. For years, my in-box has been flooded, mysteriously, with e-mails from a company that offers exotic airplane charters. My attempts to unsubscribe died out somewhere around 2010 and were replaced with resignation and a side of bitterness that comes with the fear that I'll never be able to afford watching a 70-inch flat screen on a leather sofa en route to Belize.

There are two basic types of queries:

1. **THE TRADITIONAL QUERY:** In this query, the most classic form, you're writing a letter to an editor about what you want to write. You'll include all the essentials—which we'll get into soon enough—and your hope is that an editor will respond with interest and give you a contract to write the piece.

2. **THE ON-SPEC QUERY:** Here you'll do what most writers recommend you never do (but I will!)—you'll offer the editor a free look at a complete article that has not been previously discussed with or assigned by the editor. Again, this is a polarizing topic—and one we'll dive deeper into. But for now, to further convolute things, I should add that there are three variants of on-spec queries:

   - In the first, you e-mail an editor explaining that you've written an article you think would fit the publication, and you invite the editor to take a look at it.
   - In the second, you briefly explain your concept to the editor and then include the full piece below your explanation.
   - In the third, you explain the article that you *want* to write and then offer to write it for the editor on spec, without a contract, if she is interested in the concept.

GAME ON

Now let's play a game. I'll include a variant of a query we received below, and you tell me if we bought it or not:

> To the Editors of Writer's Digest:
> As writers, we love hearing and reading the war stories of our peers, which come laden with wisdoms of their own.
> I have a literal war story for you: I would like to offer you "Being a War Journalist." This 4,000-word feature will recap my one-year journey into the genre. I began as an unpublished writer slinging queries around and ended up finding myself on a fully paid, year-long solo journey around the world, and writing about it for a slew of magazines.

```
    This piece will display how I did it, and most impor-
tant, my personal insights into war, which will be the
core of the piece.
    My words and images have appeared in [redacted].
    I look forward to hearing from you.

Thank you,
[redacted]
```

What do you think? Did we buy it, or no?

… We did not.

What's wrong with it?

Very little, actually. It's intriguing. It hooks me immediately and makes me want to learn more—how'd he go from unpublished to this amazing trek, and what did he discover along the way? It contains no deadly grammar sins or any unforgivable all-caps treatments. It opens with a valid touch point for writers. It includes mention of his other publications.

It's all right.

But, naturally, being an editor, I have to nitpick. It's too short; it needs more details. It could have preserved the intrigue factor while giving me a better clue as to what sort of article he's actually proposing. It should be addressed to an actual person. The proposed article is too long and falls outside the realm of WD's word count, which is stated in the magazine's submission guidelines. I've never been a fan of the Courier New font.[10]

But the critical flaw, and the reason it ended in a nice rejection letter is WD is a how-to magazine. There are venues that publish work like this (and I'd like to read this article in one of those), but a piece in which the core of the story is the writer's personal insights into war is not a fit for the type of content WD publishes.

I promise that's the last time I'll flog the "never pitch something that a publication does not publish" pony. It's time that horse went to pasture. The main reason I wanted to include this one here, though, is that it goes to show that even a decent query can end in rejection if you don't do your homework first.

Now, let's trot out a new horse.

---

10 See? Editors suck. They're crabby and subjective and irritable.

Hey,

Just wanted to shoot you a couple article ideas for the magazine …

IDEA #1: HOW I CONNED WRITERS DIGEST INTO LETTING ME WRITE FOR THEM … and How You Can Do the Same Thing (but maybe not with Writers Digest)

and …

IDEA #2: HOW TO FAKE YOUR WAY THROUGH YOUR FIRST BOOK PROPOSAL

I'm attaching a little "info sheet" with my pitches for them. If you like them, I'd love to do either or both … maybe for different issues.
If you don't like them … never talk to me again.
Lemme know what you think!

Chad

Did we buy either one?

Admittedly, this is a bit of a trick query. It came from Chad Gervich, who had been writing for *Writer's Digest* for years. But it displays why we hired him in the first place:

1. He gets to the point fast.
2. He offers two succinct ideas that could work for the magazine and backs them up with an info sheet fleshing them out with further details.
3. He baits the hook and piques my interest.
4. He lets his personality show. Now, granted, you probably wouldn't want to let this much personality show in your initial contact with a publication, but giving an editor a taste of the voice she can expect in an article is akin to those delightful food samples big-box stores strategically plant around the aisles on a Saturday. Even if an editor doesn't like what's being served, she gets a taste of the real deal and that can inform her decision. You never know: An editor may absolutely love your voice. After seeing endless queries locked up in straightjackets, the frank, funny ones are often the queries that stand out for me. Don't forget that there's an actual person on the other end of the line when you're drafting a query.

A QUERY, DECONSTRUCTED

Now that we're getting deeper into the pitch thicket, let's take a look at a breakdown of a solid query.

A QUERY SHOULD START WITH A SHORT, PUNCHY INTRO, LIKE A *LOGLINE*. In the screenwriting world, a logline is a one-sentence description of a script that's so strong and so high-concept that it effectively captures the heart of the story. (A logline is used to sell your screenplay to the person in charge, who will use it to convince his higher-ups to make the film, who will then use it to sell the film to audiences—and on and on until you're a millionaire.) My colleague and *Guide to Literary Agents* editor Chuck Sambuchino often cites these strong loglines when discussing the subject:

> To track down a serial killer, an ambitious female FBI agent-in-training seeks help from an imprisoned psychiatrist, who is both a manipulative genius and a serial killer himself. (*The Silence of the Lambs*)

> Thirty years after he failed to save President Kennedy, a veteran Secret Service agent must stop a psychopathic assassin from killing the president. (*In the Line of Fire*)

> After being kicked out of their sport for fighting, two rival male figure skaters must join forces to compete in a pairs skating competition. (*Blades of Glory*)

Loglines are also useful for pitching novels, for obvious reasons. (You use it to hook the literary agent, who uses it to hook an editor, who uses it to hook his publishing board, who uses it to hook book distributors and market it to audiences.)

So what the heck does a logline have to do with a nonfiction query for a simple article?

It's all about clarity of concept. If you can hone your idea to a compelling and concise sentence that wholly entrances an editor, then your work is basically done in thirty words. The rest of the query is gravy. The first sentence is the most important in the query—if it's good enough, it's what will inspire an editor to fish your query out of the mire that is the slush pile, clean the mud off it, and realize she's potentially found one hell of a gem.

Of course, coming up with such a killer lede isn't easy. It takes thought and skill to boil down your query to its strongest essence and to identify what would truly be most appealing to the publication, and thus would best suit its readership.

But it gets easier—and faster—as you go along and begin to develop a radar for tracking down those elusive hooks. This section will give you some insight into how to develop the skill.

A QUERY SHOULD BE TO THE POINT AND SHOULD MATCH THE TONE OF THE PUBLICATION. Never ramble in a query. A query that goes on for ten pages and is longer than the article the author is proposing causes high blood pressure in editors. If you can't express your idea succinctly in one page or less, an editor is not going to trust you to be able to write a concise article for his publication. A query reveals a lot about a freelancer's writing. Avoid the "everything but the kitchen sink" query, and don't weigh down your query with unnecessary verbiage and detail.

Also, try to channel the voice and tone of the publication in your query. Don't sacrifice your own voice in order to ape the publication's, but adapt it to their voice so they can begin to understand how you would fit into the mix.

Voices vary a great deal. Think of the down-to-earth, youthful voice of *Rolling Stone*. Now think of the stuffier, straightforward tone of *The Washington Post*. Think of the gossipy exclamation-point-ridden copy of *People*. Think of the highbrow, tweed-vest–wearing voice of *Harper's Magazine*. No voice is a better voice, but each one is unique to a publication. So, again, read the publication first and know the degree of ventriloquism your query (and subsequent article) will require.

Can't quite pin down a publication's voice? There are a few key areas in a magazine that will give you some big clues. Flip to the editor's letter or staff editorial. Study the tone, the verbiage, the presentation. A publication is crafted around an editor's vision, which is then carried throughout the book. *Writer's Digest* presents itself in an optimistic, writer-to-writer voice. *HOW* magazine presents itself as a helpful big sister for the graphic design audience. *Print* magazine takes a more advanced tone and is often more blunt, academic, and (dare I say?) pretentious. All of these tones can be found in the publications' respective editor's letters.

For further clues, take the audience into account. A publication will very often provide its media kit online for potential advertisers. The kit will contain demographic information, giving direct insights into who will be reading your article. Is your narrative nonfiction piece about a rogue, foul-mouthed boutique owner a bit too edgy for a publication with an audience consisting mostly of grandmothers?

Also, take the advertisers into account. They've obsessively studied these demographics and have determined that it's worth their money to pay to present their products and services to a publication's audience. Flip through the ads, and see what they tell you. Does the magazine contain advertisements for $10,000 watches? The guy wearing it is who you're writing to. Does the magazine have ads for the Clapper? Hip boutiques in a city? Breast augmentation? The people who want these things are, for better or worse, the ones you're writing to. Adjust your tone and approach accordingly.

A QUERY SHOULD EXPLAIN TO AN EDITOR HOW YOUR AR-TICLE WILL BENEFIT READERS. This, at the end of the day, is key. Regardless of whether you're writing how-to content or a profile of an athlete, an editor perusing your query will constantly be asking how it will serve his audience. That's his main job: to serve the audience. If an audience is served properly, it will grow. And when it grows, advertisers come or remain on board, assignments go out to freelancers, and the publication circle of life is complete.

For that reason it's best to always clearly and directly explain up front how your proposed piece will serve the audience. Once you've identified who the majority of readers are, you can then easily add a line or two justifying the piece:

> This article will directly serve *Writer's Digest*'s core audience of aspiring novelists by teaching them to …

Or …

> This article, similar to the thrilling tech-world narrative saga [name of piece] that ran in the February 2015 issue of *Wired*, will provide your audience with …

Or …

> Let's face it: *People* magazine readers want a deeper look at the trending celebrity crime sagas that captivate audiences today. My article will take a thrilling dive into …

As editors, we're obsessed with the benefit our readers will receive from your piece. So don't make an editor wonder. Tell him up front.

A QUERY SHOULD INCLUDE CONCRETE EXAMPLES AND A VERY BRIEF OUTLINE OF WHAT YOU'RE PROPOSING, SHOULD THE TOPIC WARRANT IT. Editors weep into their $7 black coffees when a piece they commissioned hits their desk in terrible shape and barely reflects the query a writer proposed. For that reason, they're highly suspicious of overly vague queries that leave them wondering just how the hell a writer will pull off this article. For instance:

> This article will teach you everything you need to know to write a novel.

Or …

> This article will tell readers how to fully wire their houses for an epic Christmas light display.

Big claims. Editors will wonder: *Does the writer know what he's talking about? How could he possibly cover that in a 750-word article? Am I going to get burned on this piece?*

I've passed on a lot of queries offering potentially great articles because a writer couldn't provide the info I needed to be able to trust him. When articles come in shoddy or unusable, it puts the editor in a bad spot. Suddenly she has a hole in her publication that she needs to fill *fast*.

To calm a nervous editor's tender mind, always include specific examples in your query. For that article about how to write a novel, you could say that you'll first tackle the most essential elements of outlining. Then you'll address the three-act structure. You'll include practical info on avoiding wooden dialogue. And on and on. A few bullet points like this will help an editor understand that your piece is indeed feasible, and let her trust that the topic is safely in your hands and that she won't be scrambling to DEFCON 5 at the eleventh hour to fill a six-page gap.

A QUERY SHOULD EXPLAIN WHY YOU'RE THE BEST—AND ONLY—PERSON TO WRITE THE PIECE YOU'RE PROPOSING.

Again, one of the key goals in querying is to get an editor to trust that you can execute on your article. Why should he believe that you can write a piece on a new Mars lander? Well, because you're a lifelong science junkie and have been studying Mars for twenty years. Why should an editor trust you to write an article on a hip new restaurant that's opening downtown? Because you're a foodie with an excellent blog and your passion lies in covering new restaurants like this one. Why should an editor trust you to write an essay on addiction? Because you were an addict for ten years.

Tell an editor why you're the best person for the job. Leverage your expertise and passion.

> As an insider for years at a top trading firm, I know how financial deals like this one work. I know who to interview. And I know how to break it all down for your readers so that anyone can understand
> ...

A QUERY SHOULD INCLUDE A PROPOSED WORD COUNT.

Simple enough: Just tell an editor how long you envision the piece will be, so she can start to visualize it within the publication. That will let her know the scope of the piece and will also give her some clues into whether the query has legs.

For instance, a writer proposes a personality profile of Leonardo DiCaprio ... at 500 words. That would be way too short for a catch like DiCaprio. But, more important, how much can you really learn about a well-known subject like DiCaprio in a mere 500 words?

Or, a writer proposes a 6,000-word piece about a new restaurant with no crazy hook other than the fact that the restaurant is, well, new. Six thousand words is far too long for something like that (just like 2,000 words is way too long for a movie review in the form of an apology letter from Jackie Chan to viewers).

While proposed word counts are important, they're not a crucial factor in whether you'll get accepted or rejected (assuming you don't pitch a forty-five-word interview with Leonardo DiCaprio). You're merely giving an editor a glimpse into what you're envisioning. If an editor likes what she sees, she'll adapt it to a space she has open. If you pitch a 1,500-word story that an editor likes, she may see if you can do an 800-word version of it for the front of the book. If an editor thinks your piece may fit well into a feature package she has on the horizon, she may ask if you can make the 1,500-word pitch into a 3,000-word story.

Word count is a highly malleable—and highly negotiable—factor. Before you pitch, be sure to check the publication's submission guidelines to see what lengths they specify. If they don't include length requirements, pick up a copy of the publication and do some old-fashioned calculations to make sure you're shooting at the right target.

A QUERY SHOULD INCLUDE LINKS TO YOUR "CLIPS"—SAMPLES OF YOUR PUBLISHED WORK. Again, never include unsolicited attachments. The IT guy will come over and delete the query himself, and scold the editor for wanting to "just take a quick peep." Rather, include links to specific articles or a personal website URL that contains links and/or PDFs to your best work. (And don't think including links is all for show—we really do read clips to make sure you can practice what you pitch.)

But what if you don't have any clips? Don't despair—all hope is not lost. Here we find ourselves at one of the biggest paradoxes of freelance writing: How do you get your first clips if you have to have clips to get your first clips?[11]

First off, do you have a blog? As I mentioned earlier, I often get asked if writing you've done for blogs and websites counts as a clip. It depends on the editor. A lot of blog pieces are half finished, quickly assembled, and sloppy, giving blogging a bad name. But we've all read great blogs.

Moreover, *what the hell is considered a blog?* WordPress sites and Blogger.com sites, sure. But *Gawker* is technically a blog. So is The

---

[11] Head explodes.

Huffington Post. Blogs, like print publications, run the gamut in terms of quality and content.

If the online writing you've done directly mirrors the quality and style of what you want to propose to a publication, by all means, include it. Some writers publish fantastic pieces on their blogs because they never figured out how to crack into print, or they didn't want to waste time trying. These people often get book deals later when editors notice a blog that's taking off.

Another great strategy to breaking in without polished clips: Write on spec.

Finally, if you don't have any clips, don't call attention to that fact. Just present a rock-solid query. Once you've hooked an editor, he may ask who else you've written for. That will give you an outlet to converse with the editor and keep him from discarding your query up front for lacking clips and writing creds.

So what does all this look like in action? Let's examine a theoretical[12] dream query for a men's magazine. For purposes of classification, this one will be a traditional (not on-spec) query.

> SUBJECT: Query: What Hunter S. Thompson Taught Me About the Meaning of Life
>
> Dear John,
> He gripped the wheel. He hit the gas and turned off his headlights in the black night. Then, Hunter S. Thompson began to tell me about the meaning of life. ❶
>
> I'd like to propose a 3,000-word ❷ narrative feature for your annual "Meaning of Everything" issue. ❸
>
> When I was twenty-two, a chance encounter with the legendary writer at a diner led me on one of the most bizarre—and profound—nights of my life. It was 2 A.M. Thompson, whom I had met about twenty minutes earlier, threw his beer bottle across the parking lot and headed to his '71 Impala convertible. Then, he turned and asked if I wanted to go for a ride. I got in. He threw a weathered pad of paper at me and said, "You may want to take notes."❹
>
> I did. And throughout the course of the night Thompson shared his wisdoms and philosophies on everything from books to drugs

---

12 Totally made up. Though I wish it were real.

to his past, his future, and, yes, the topic that dominated the night: the meaning of life.

I have never written about this experience before, and I think it would be an ideal fit for the issue. While I'm proposing it as a narrative that reveals the story of the night to showcase Thompson's thoughts, I'd be happy to reconfigure it in any way that you feel would be most meaningful to your readers.

As a freelancer with ten years of experience writing for magazines, newspapers and everything in between (see www.URL.com), I believe it's finally time to share this story, and I think this issue would be the perfect venue.

Many thanks in advance for your consideration.

[Name]

❶ Compelling lede. At least, I think so.

❷ Word count: Check.

❸ Conveys knowledge of publication.

❹ Written in the style of the publication.

❺ Conveys the benefits for readers.

❻ Conveys openness and adaptability.

❼ Shows why she's the best person to write it.

Now, let's take a look at another real query.

Dear Zachary,

There are times when writers feel their muse bursting forth—words flow out into sentences, paragraphs, and chapters. But there are other times each word typed is agony. Understanding the dynamics of each and how they relate to the final writing product will help writers capitalize on inspiration and push through perspiration.

In an article entitled, "The Paradox of Inspiration and Perspiration," I help writers understand:

- The Pinch Hitter Reality: Pinch hitters have the same statistics whether they're batting in a stressful situation or whether it's the top of the first. In other words, it's the writer's patient dedication to the craft in the mundane (perspiration) that fosters brilliance (inspiration).
- Not to trust emotions: Many writers I surveyed for this article found their best, least-edited work came from

their hard won words. They might've *felt* each sentence
lacked luster, but that feeling didn't confirm the reality of
the final product.

- BOC (Butt on Chair) = Eventual inspiration. Several novelists queried reported they started their writing day by
  sheer determination, only to have the words flow after
  they warmed up.

My articles have appeared in *The Writer, Marriage Partnership, In
Touch* and *Kindred Spirit.* My books include: *Authentic Parenting
in a Postmodern Culture, Watching the Tree Limbs* (Christy Final-
ist), and *Wishing on Dandelions.* I have three novels and a memoir
slated to release in 2009 and 2010 through HarperCollins. I am the
owner of The Writers View, a 1300-member online professional
writing group, and I pen a well-trafficked blog for new writers
(www.wannabepublished.blogspot.com). I'm a book mentor at The
Writing Spa (www.thewritingspa.com). And I've taught writing at
several major writing conferences (400+ writers).

Would *Writer's Digest* be interested in "The Paradox of Inspiration and Perspiration"? A 1,000-word draft is available upon request.

Warmly,
Mary E. DeMuth

What do you think about this query? Did we buy it?

We did!

But not for the reasons you might think.

Sure, it's a solid query: It has a compelling hook. It's not too short,
and it's not too long. It covers the main points of the proposed piece. It
includes mention of her extensive writing experience.

Still, truth be told, when I first read this query I was on the fence.
WD gets a lot of pitches like this, and sooner or later, they all start to feel
too familiar—and if we're sensing it as editors, our readers will, too. You
don't want to get stale by publishing the same pieces issue after issue.
In this case, we had run something similar a couple of issues back.

But then she includes that magic line at the end: *A 1,000-word draft
is available upon request.*

In this case, it meant the difference between an acceptance and a
rejection. I had nothing to lose, so I said sure, send it on over. And when

she did, I realized the piece was totally different than what I was antici-pating based on our previous article—and immediately bought it.

As I wrote earlier, this is the power of on-spec writing: *It lets your writing speak for itself.*

Especially if you're a writer without clips, writing on spec can be a deal-maker with an editor. You don't have to convince her of anything. Just write an amazingly great piece, and get it in front of her. Your prose will do the talking.

Have trouble fully articulating your idea in a one-pager? I do, too. Write on spec.

Have a piece in mind that would be easier to write than the query letter itself? Write on spec.

Of course, writing on spec draws ire from many writers. As the Jok-er said in *The Dark Knight*, "If you're good at something, never do it for free"—and many writers refuse to budge on that point. But technically, writing on spec isn't writing for free. Writing on spec is the equivalent of putting something on the shelf of your boutique rather than provid-ing a small description in the window with a sticker that says, "Order now!" You need credibility and clout before people will feel fully com-fortable ordering your product. So a great way to start is to put it on your shelf. And for that matter, don't think only newer writers write on spec. I still occasionally do. I have enough trust in my product to be-lieve that if I put it on the shelf, an interested buyer will like what I do enough to carry it to the register.

A caveat, of course: Be smart about what you write on spec. I've been burned by it, and I know many other writers who have, too. You don't ever want to write anything on spec that requires interviews, a significant time commitment,[13] intense research and fact-checking, and the like.

I once wrote a 5,000-word profile about a notable man with a pretty amazing backstory. It played out in different acts, featured a tricky narra-tive structure, and had one of the best endings I think I've ever written.

Enthralled, and having worked on it daily after work for a month or two, I sent it to an editor of a local magazine.

---

13 Oddly and hilariously, though, this is how novel-writing works.

No response. I followed up, sheepishly. No response. Eventually I tried to submit it elsewhere. No response.

Two months down the drain on a fool's errand. Had I queried to begin with, I might have been able to solicit direct interest—and direction—from the editor, and subsequently the story might have seen the light of day. Instead I've got a hefty stack of pages in my digital filing cabinet that I simply won't let go. (I still love the thing!)[14]

Instead of such epic screeds, your on-spec pieces should be like the essays I discussed earlier—pieces with a smaller time commitment that you can pull off easily and enjoy doing.

Be responsible. Practice safe spec work.

Let's look at another one.

> Dear Mr. Petit,
>
> Robert Kirkman's writing credits have lots and lots of flesh-eating zombies and mutants, characters that have resonated in the comic book and television industries. His ongoing series *The Walking Dead*, about a post-apocalyptic world infested with the undead, is approaching its 10th year via Image Comics, also home of his coming-of-age superhero satire **Invincible**. Recently, he became partner at Image but didn't allow business to impede his writings.
>
> There's more to chew on. In mid-October, AMC launches its second season of *The Walking Dead* television series, in which he produces and writes with others. The season's second half is slated to resume in late February. *The Walking Dead* video game also launches in Fall 2011.
>
> Would you be interested in a feature on Kirkman? The story would largely center on his writing process, character development and reflections on *The Walking Dead* adapted for new audiences. Perhaps you prefer a tighter focus on writing about the undead ("Talking Dead with Robert Kirkman")? Overall, the piece would unpack the mind of a leading writer in popular (nerd) culture. For aspiring and professional writers, the takeaway is a deeper under-

---

14 Did you ever watch *Unsolved Mysteries*? If so, it's time for the satisfying follow-up story. Amazingly, about four or five years after I submitted the story, an editor from the publication called and said the editor in chief had remembered a piece I once sent them. He had liked the topic and thought it might fit a special section they had coming up. Could I do the story at 250 words? (Down from 5,000.) Of course I could! I was thrilled to be able to do it and was pumped that a fragment of it finally saw publication. However, the task of cutting 5,000 words down to 250 is a miserable saga we'll save for another day.

standing of the perils and excitement of writing in popular culture. If the story runs in March, it can also serve as a preview to San Diego Comic-Con, a rich networking opportunity for writers interested in that field.

In talking with his PR contact, Kirkman is available for interviews.

Thanks for your time,
Rich

Did we buy it?

We did!

This query, from writer and educator Rich Shivener, was very, very well executed. First, he starts off by qualifying what he's about to propose: *The Walking Dead* is a hot show that's blowing up and about to launch its second season, and Kirkman has been writing the book for ten years. Then, he includes what the meat of the story would center around, showing focus: Kirkman's writing process, his character development (one of the series' strongest points), and so on. He also directly states the takeaways for readers, which, again, helps an editor to understand why a story would be a good fit.

One thing that also helped seal the deal: Shivener indicated that he was in touch with Kirkman's PR person, and that the interview could happen if we gave the green light. This is key, because editors receive a lot of pitches that read as, "I'd like to pitch you an interview with Stephen King." But interviews with such big fish are hard to get. Pie-in-the-sky offers to interview huge names (especially actors, A-list authors, or chart-topping singers) are taken with a grain of salt because editors know how hard they can be to arrange. (I'm still waiting on a Stephen Colbert interview that a writer promised me six years ago.)

Moreover, one of the worst things a writer pitching a publication can do is to say, "I'd like to interview [insert famous name here]." ... Why would you like to interview him? What would the hook be? Do you really have access to this person?

Shivener's query is a good place to make a confession that most editors keep secret and would only admit over their eighth bourbon. In the original query (before I cleaned up a couple of areas) there were a few small grammatical errors.[15] Some editors will say that they'll make the query into a paper airplane at that point and send it out the window.

Sure, you should always make sure your query is 100-percent top-notch before you send it.

But if you do make a couple of errors, as we all do on occasion, it doesn't matter.

The idea at the core of this pitch and the structure of the query were so good that the last thing I cared about was a tiny error.

Editors are supposed to edit and fix things. I'd much rather correct a misspelling in a beautiful, well-structured piece than be stuck with a turd of an article that is beyond repair.

All of this is to say the idea is what matters most, not the vehicle it's in. Queries, like great writing, are anything but surface level.

On the flip side, there's this query:

> Hello,
> I would like to propose a series of four "how-to" articles for Writer's Digest Magazine.
> I am the author of … [redacted].
> I have four ideas. They are:
>
> "Improve your fiction now"
> "Writing the best parts of your novel"
> "How to make fiction"
> "Plots—how to get in there and write them"
>
> …
>
> Thanks.
> [redacted]

I don't need to tell you whether we bought any of these. Unfortunately this breed of query is all too common—especially when it comes to niche magazines specializing in highly specific topics. The scenario goes like this: A writer will hear, in this case, "writing magazine." Then, he'll blast off a series of overly broad ideas. This was the case at WD, just like it's the case at tech magazines, which likely receive a weekly flood of queries for articles titled "How to Be Good at Twitter."

---

15 Next time I see him he'll probably punch me for this.

In every query you write, assume that every angle has already been taken. Your challenge is to come up with something totally new, something totally fresh. *Writer's Digest*, which has been around for ninety-plus years, has covered all the core topics of writing in every way imaginable. How are you going to provide a fresh insight into an old topic? *Family Tree Magazine* has covered genealogy in every way imaginable. How are you going to provide a fresh insight into an old topic? Same with *Horticulture* and flowers. Same with *Numismatics News* and coins.

It can seem like a tall order, but it's really not. Every writer is imbued with a talent, outlook, and ideation process that is uniquely his, and it's just a matter of channeling it.

For instance, for WD's annual novel issue, a great writer pitched the publication a piece about how to incorporate facts and research into fiction. She had a research background and presented a solid and interesting way to broach the subject of authenticity in fiction.

One final note on that last sample query: In general, it's been said that you should never include more than two ideas in any single query. I'll go the extra picky mile and add that, in my opinion, you should never include more than one.

Why?

Ninety-five percent of the time, queries like this are akin to shooting from the hip. They contain a set of vague, untargeted ideas, none of which is strong enough to stand on its own. Each idea dilutes the potential strength of the others.

So keep things focused. Take one idea and fully develop it to the point that it'll leave the editor drooling for more as opposed to groaning because it feels like she's picking from a subpar list of combos at Denny's.

Let's take a look at one more—and then I'll share one of the most painful queries I've ever received.

> Dear Sir or Madame,[16]
> I'd love to submit an article to WD. Your editorial mission of being a publication "of writers helping writers" has always deeply resonated with me, and I think I could make a meaningful contribution to it.

---

16 Inclusive!

I'd like to propose "Accepting the Rejection," an 800-word instructional article informing readers how to properly accept—and come to terms with—rejection letters.

I've received my own. I've also had a lot of anti-rejection letters, and have found publication in a variety of outlets—even those who have previously published my work.

I'd like to share with your readers the proper way to navigate the rejection waters, with an eye on landing work in that particular publication in the future.

Thank you for your consideration,
[Redacted]

Did we buy it?

We didn't. But again, probably not for the reasons you might think. Sure, the query was sparse. It gave little indication of what would be included in the subsequent article. But there was a factor of intrigue to it. The topic of rejection is (unfortunately) familiar to writers. Stories about rejection can be great reads, especially if the writer spun it for the positive and landed his work in the publications that were rejecting him. There could be lessons there.

But ultimately, we rejected this query for the same reason that we reject 95 percent of the queries that come in: We had run a somewhat similar essay on the topic of rejection only one issue back.

Query overlap—writers who get to the prize first—is your biggest enemy as a freelancer.

So how can you fight it?

First, always, *always* search the topic that you're proposing on the publication's website before you draft your query. If they've recently covered it and it isn't a truly evergreen topic that can run every issue, your query is likely to get rejected, whether it's about a beauty tip or a celebrity profile.

To go a step further, search your topic on the publication's competitors' websites. Have they recently run a story on this topic? If so, again, your target publication might be hesitant to breach the topic (unless it's evergreen). Nobody wants to look like they're a day late to the party or to seem as if they're simply aping the competition.

Now, that being said, it's high time for a disclaimer.

For the past 10,000 words, you've listened to me ramble about the subject of queries—all the amazingly vast things you should do, all the amazingly vast things you should not do. You may be wondering: *Why the hell are there so many rules to a simple one-page letter, and what the hell is the point of even sending one if there are so many constraints?*

You make a valid point. Query writing can seem discouraging, if not Sisyphean. But don't let it consume you. There's no way to follow all of these steps 100 percent. To do so, you'd have to transmit your consciousness into an editor's brain to know exactly what he's looking for and what he's already acquired for forthcoming issues.

But by simply having all of these rules and elements in the back of your mind, you'll be drastically ahead of the curve compared to all the other freelancers. Remember when I was telling you about the true state of a slush pile? It's not a pretty place. Those who follow the elements throughout this chapter will rise to the top.

RANDOM BASICS

On that note, let's discuss a few more random query basics that'll help you stand out.

WORK THE SALINGER ULTIMATUM

First off, the best thing you can do as a freelancer is offer a publication something they can't get on their own. At WD, I used to tell people that if they had an "in" with the great recluse writer J.D. Salinger, I'd pay them out of pocket then and there for the interview.[17]

But it goes beyond that. Again, channel your expertise. What do you have that a publication's staff and stable of regular writers don't? What expert qualifications do you possess that you could translate into an assignment? Being writers, nobody on the WD staff has ever had any actual knowledge of math. Seriously, I need a calculator to decipher a 20 percent tip. Seeing an editor try to carry numbers is highly effec-

---

17 This is, of course, when J.D. Salinger was still alive. I'd have given them my credit cards for an interview from beyond the grave.

tive comedy. So when a tax expert writer (oxymoron?) came to WD to pitch "Taxpertise for Writers," we gladly took her up on the offer. (The downside is that it took me weeks and a gallon of tears to fact-check.)

PLAY THE GAME

Don't forget the basics. Always write your query in AP Style. Always write your query in clean, sparkling prose, and be cordial and friend-ly—even if the editor is a jerk, or you get your own "What the hell?" re-sponse. Journalism is an amazingly incestuous business, and we all seem to know each other in one way or another, be it at a cocktail party, a conference, or from sharing the same staff or writers at one point or another. And we all talk. You never want to burn a bridge in this busi-ness, and you never know when the editor you're rude to at one publica-tion will hop over to the editorial team of another you'd love to pitch.

Further, never, ever trash an editor on social media or a blog, no matter how much he or she deserves it. It's just not worth it. Most edi-tors (whether out of narcissism or curiosity) have Google Alerts set up on their names, which means that whenever anyone mentions them anywhere on the Internet, they get a notification and a link. After re-jecting queries (in my very nice and polite way, I might add), I've been called everything from a "dumbass" to a "dullard." While I built up a strong rejection threshold of my own long ago, I still get little rage spikes whenever it happens. On our end, rejection is never personal. And it shouldn't be on the writer's part, either. Avoid the bitterness, chalk it up to the game, and move on to the next market.

BE LIKE RICK STEVES

Now, here's where I'm really going to draw some ire from my col-leagues: If you're having trouble breaking into a publication, offer to write a piece for the publication for *free*. Yes, I said it: free! The anti-on-spec'ers have already caught wind of that sentence, have collected their pitchforks, and are outside my house, calling for my head. Before I grab my bug-out bag[18] and flee through a series of underground tun-

---

[18] Consisting largely of bourbon and pens.

nels constructed specifically for such scenarios, allow me a few moments to defend myself.

Many publications contain sections in which random readers and writers sound off on a variety of issues. *Newsweek* long had its "My Turn" column. Many newspapers and weeklies have a "Last Word"-style section in which readers riff on a topic important to them. They're like expanded op-eds but with much more cred—it's the type of piece that transcends "letter to the editor" and becomes a validated clip.

The nice thing about sections like this is they're usually written by nonwriters. So when you, as a writer, send a submission in for them, the editor is often pleasantly surprised by the caliber of the work and, more often than not, will run your piece.

Now, often, these sections don't pay. So why would a writer waste her time on them? For very good reason. Freelancing is a long-term game. The goal is not to get a $100 check. The goal is to develop a *relationship*—a theme we'll revisit throughout this book. Your goal in your first contact with a publication is to lay the foundation for this relationship and to get your foot in the door. Once you've had your writing accepted and published in this free section, you then have leeway to casually throw out to your new editor, "Thanks so much for publishing the piece. Loved the way it looked in print. And by the way, I'd be remiss if I didn't add that I'm also a freelance writer and am currently taking on assignments. I'd love to contribute more to your publication." The door is open, you're past the slush pile, and you're on your way to more assignments.

I've done exactly this, and it has led to a series of fruitful relationships. All I had to do to break the ice was write a simple essay—which, nerdily, is something I find to be quite fun—and eat the cost of the first piece. Many other writers I know have done the same thing.

This is even how television personality and travel guru Rick Steves got his start. He offered his shows free to public channels around the country, because he knew the longer game was to build a *brand* versus achieving one sale. Today he runs a multimillion-dollar travel empire and gets to do what he loves every day.

Again, it should be noted here that when I say "publication," I don't mean it literally. Web properties—and their often zero-sum budgets—count, too.

So write for free, haters be damned. Simply put, writing for free often pays off.

DO NOT CHANNEL YOUR INNER C-3PO

Talk to an editor on a human level. Appeal to her as a person. When writers respond to an editor and seem like stiff robots or treat editors like royalty, it sets a weird tone. Instead, be normal. Of course set a professional tone, but don't be afraid to reflect the editor's personality back at her, especially if it's in a humorous tone. Converse with her and thank her for looking at your query—even if you get rejected. Remember, the goal is to establish a relationship. And the best way to begin is to connect with her as a person. Leave a positive impression for the next query.

WAITING FOR YOUR EDITOR, GODOT

As for follow-up, this can be a tricky line to walk. Most submission guidelines state how long an editor has to respond to you, and they often state how and when to follow up if you haven't heard back. Personally, I go about a week and a half to two weeks before following up. Any shorter, and you risk annoying the editor. Any longer, and you risk being forgotten. Keep it short and sweet:

> Hello Jane,
>
> I hope all is well your way. I'm writing to follow up on my query "How to Write a Book About Freelancing," attached below. Do you have any interest in the piece for your March issue, which covers writing books about freelancing?
>
> Many thanks in advance for your time and consideration.
>
> Zac
>
> --
>
> Zachary Petit
> Writer Extraordinaire

POP THE QUESTION

Regardless of whether you get accepted or rejected, ask for the publication's editorial calendar. Some publications release them, and some don't. But if you can get your hands on it, it's worth its weight in gold. An editorial calendar summarizes what the publication will be publishing in the next year—issue themes, big article topics, etc. At every magazine I've worked for, we've created them in the summer. Ad reps use them to sell ads to clients. Editors use them to solicit articles directly related to their planned coverage. Some go into more detail than others, but the key value in having them is that you can target your pitches to what the publication will be covering—giving you a direct bull's-eye to aim for, and putting you in the catbird seat, where you can relax, sip a mimosa, and look at all the untargeted queries in the slush pile grasping for a place at the table.

To give you an idea of what you might see in an editorial calendar, here's what I put together for *Print* magazine in 2015:

FEBRUARY: TYPOGRAPHY TODAY + LEGENDS IN ADVERTISING

In this issue, *Print* tackles one of its readers' most passionate topics: Typography. We'll take a deep dive into how type has evolved—where it has been in the past, major industry milestones and so on—and analyze current trends to decode where it's going tomorrow. Moreover, we'll find out who is taking it there by naming the most innovative new typographers and offering an in-depth look at their stunning work. The February issue will also delve into the world of advertising and will feature some of the best work being done today as we announce the winners of *Print*'s Legends in Advertising Awards.

SPECIAL FOCUS: Typography + Stock Photography

SPRING: *PRINT'S* 75TH ANNIVERSARY ISSUE + DESIGN HISTORY

Since its debut in 1940, *Print* has been on the cutting edge of the world of design, and in doing so, has documented the history and evolution of the entire field. This issue will honor that legacy by celebrating the history of design—both our own, and the legends of the field, from Paul Rand to Saul Bass to Gordon Lippincott to Charles Eames (who have all written for *Print* and appeared within its pages over the years). In addition, *Print* at seventy-five will debut an exciting new lineup of columns, covering everything from stirring profiles of modern designers to a new offering from design guru Debbie Millman.

> **SPECIAL FOCUS:** Illustration + Paper + Printing
> **OFFICIAL ISSUE OF:** HOW Interactive Design Conference

SUMMER: THE NEW VISUAL ARTISTS ISSUE + DESIGN TRENDS + DESIGN SCHOOLS

Every year, *Print* collects nominations from top art directors, industry vets and designers to select our prestigious and highly anticipated class of New Visual Artists—the top twenty designers under thirty. A long-standing unique honor in the field, in this issue the New Visual Artists (who come from a vast array of backgrounds and design specialties, from illustration to typography to interactive design) are profiled, giving insight into how they became the designers they are today, from the schools they attended to their current firms. In addition to featuring cutting-edge designers who often go on to become stars (such as former NVA Jessica Walsh), this issue will capture and report on prominent design trends today, and what will shape the field tomorrow, alongside these brilliant artists.

> **SPECIAL FOCUS:** Design Schools + Job & Career Advice

FALL: DESIGNING A BETTER WORLD

Here *Print* takes a look at the true transformative power of design and poses the question: What's broken in our world that design could fix? From societal problems to building better street signs and safety packaging, *Print* will profile organizations and artists seeking to solve a variety of issues through design—and will also commission a set of designers to each tackle a different problem by generating exclusive redesigns or prototype concepts. This issue will spotlight the fact that design is about far more than being aesthetically pleasing—and that the role it can have in solving crucial issues runs vast and deep.

> **SPECIAL FOCUS:** Sustainability + Stock Photography

WINTER: REGIONAL DESIGN ANNUAL + DESIGNER OF THE YEAR

The December issue will feature an expanded page count to give full coverage to our most popular issue of the year, and the most respected design annual in the industry: The Regional Design Annual. Now in its thirty-fifth year, the RDA serves as a stunning catalog of the most innovative work being done coast-to-coast in the United States (by region), featuring everything from illustration to advertising to posters to annual reports. The issue also features roundups of the best book covers, album covers, and apps of 2015, and offers cultural design insight into the regions featured in the RDA. For the first time, *Print* will also confer with top names in the industry and select one designer to be named the most impactful designer of the year. A profile on this designer and his or her achievements and contributions to the field in 2015 and throughout his or her career will be featured.

SPECIAL FOCUS: Regional Design Annual + Best of the Year Coverage (Books, Apps, Albums) + Designer of the Year

IF YOU LOVE AN EDITOR, SET HIM FREE

Finally, a word of biased, personal advice: Avoid the phenomenon known as the immediate requery—when an editor rejects a writer's pitch, and the writer sends off another idea to the editor seconds later. Now, many writers will tell you to always do the immediate requery, mistakenly thinking that you must send another query "while you've got the editor on the line." This is absolutely false and bad advice, the main reason being that it usually leads to bad, shot-from-the-hip queries, such as the one earlier in this chapter that led to four watered-down, unusable ideas. Statistically speaking (and not from simply being a curmudgeon), I can honestly say that I don't think I've ever accepted an immediate requery, simply because I haven't ever received a good one.

If you're truly afraid that an editor won't remember you when you query him again later, here's what you should do: Take some time to think, and process the best idea that you feel will be a great fit for the publication. Then, take some time to develop the query and polish it up so that it's at its best. Then, when you're ready to present it to the editor, simply respond in-line with your last query (responding to the original thread with the editor). The editor will remember you, your idea, and your correspondence, and nothing will have been lost in the translation.

THE END

Before I bring this massive chapter to a close, allow me a moment to share with you one particular query gem I've received.

> Dear Zack,
> I have a story idea to share with you. One that will make your magazine better. Your magazine as you probably know is not good at all. I'm here to help you fix that. In my piece …
>
> [Redacted]

Come on! That's like the freelance copyeditor who will eviscerate a copy of a publication with red pen and send it to an editor with a "you need me—hire me" note. That may be true. But it's sure as hell not going to happen.

So my final piece of advice on querying: Don't be the writer who causes an editor to create a blacklist folder.

Overall, there's no 100-percent winning mix for a great query, and some of the best queries break the rules listed throughout this chapter. But if you follow the basic tenets of good querying, present yourself in a professional manner, don't call an editor's work stupid, and focus on building the foundations of a strong partnership with the publication, you'll be vastly above all of the other submissions in the slush pile and well on your way to seeing your words printed in your publication of choice.

CHAPTER 6

TALKING THE TALK

"I think the deeper you go into questions, the deeper or more interesting the questions get. And I think that's the job of art."

—ANDRE DUBUS III

"We journalists love writing about eccentrics. We hate writing about impenetrable, boring people. It makes us look bad: The duller the interviewee, the duller the prose. If you want to get away with wielding true, malevolent power, be boring."

—JON RONSON, *THE PSYCHOPATH TEST*

If a publication has accepted your query and has given you an assignment, there's a very good chance you'll now have to talk the talk: You'll have to interview a source, or multiple sources, for your story.

Some people dread interviewing. Others love it. It probably depends on whether you're an introvert or an extrovert. But don't worry about such differences. While interviewing may come easier to extroverts, anyone can do it. As a proud introvert, it wasn't the easiest thing in the world to start a reporting job that required me to interview people day in and day out. But I quickly developed a style, and you can, too.

To start, there are three basic types of interviews:

1. The in-person interview
2. The telephone interview (or, as is becoming increasingly common, the Skype interview)
3. The e-mail interview

The type of interview you conduct will depend heavily on the type of story you're writing, who you're interviewing, and your access to that person.

Let's begin with a quick examination of each type of interview. Then, we'll jump back to the specifics of how to successfully pull them off.

THE IN-PERSON INTERVIEW

Many classic (and smart) journalists regard this as the perfection of the form, and for good reason. For obtaining details, the best interaction, and the best results, nothing beats an in-person interview. It may seem like a huge pain in the ass: You have to pitch the story, get it accepted, contact your interviewee, set up a time to meet with the interviewee, record your conversation, transcribe your notes, make sense of it all, and then write the thing up. But don't think of interviewing in person as going the extra mile. In the long run, if you really want to write a great story, *this method will save you time.*

As I said before, I love to write profiles. But I despise writing profiles based on phone interviews. You can't capture a person's essence over a telephone or broadband connection. You can *try* (and, believe me, I have, many times—it's not every day that a magazine will fly you very far to interview a source), but you'll find yourself struggling to draw some deep human insights about a subject. The writing, and the potential quality of your story, will be deeply impacted by the type of interview you do. With profiles, meeting in person can also be key to constructing a great narrative. Rather than rehashing, say, a celebrity's life, the more interesting story often unfolds when a writer tags along with him in some manner and builds a story within the story—she goes jogging with George Clooney, for instance, or shopping for art supplies with Thomas Kincaid. And there's no other way you could get a story like that than by being with your subject face to face.

Of course, not every story is a profile. But that doesn't mean in-person interviews aren't great for most other types of pieces. If you're doing a Q&A, you'll not only be able to interact with your source and offer meaningful responses and follow-up questions, but you'll also be able to examine the source firsthand, which can generate valuable insights for the introduction that will inevitably precede your Q&A content.

If you're writing a news story, you'll find that it's a lot more difficult for officials and others to ... um ... err ... *bend the truth*[1] to your face. Any reporter worth her salt can see right through a line of BS, but it's much easier to do so in person than it is on the phone or—*gasp!*—via e-mail.

If you're writing an article about a tragedy that has occurred, there is no more powerful experience than being in the same room with a source and connecting on a human level with him.

If you're writing an article about a chef's new recipe, what better place to be than in her kitchen, observing as she blends ingredients and sautés vegetables?

If a source doesn't want to open up or talk to you—but you need him to—it's a lot harder for that source to throw you out of his house than it is to hang up on you.

I don't think I'm wildly old-school for believing that in-person interviews are generally best. I can say from the experience of thousands of interviews that they truly are. But. I can also say from thousands of interviews that practicality must be taken into consideration. You're not always able to link up with a source in person. Simple as that.

If that's the case, it's time to reach for the phone.

---

[1] Lie!

THE PHONE INTERVIEW

As anyone who has ever called (or tried to call) me probably knows, I'm the type of person who genuinely hates talking on the phone. I much prefer direct interactions and being able to see people's eyes, read them, and respond to them. I hate losing the nuances of a conversation over the wire. That said, phone interviews have a time and a place, and have often saved the day for me. Again, regardless of whether you hate interviewing people in person or are at the opposite end of the spectrum and hate talking on the phone, these skills can be picked up, honed, and employed. I have a whole persona and mentality that I snap into when I'm chatting with sources over the phone, and the more you interview, the more you'll develop your own.

Phone interviews are the journalist's savior when you need one of those supplementary quotes that don't quite merit an in-person meeting. When it comes to newspaper stories and news articles (and, being honest, most pieces), you'll generally need at least three sources to fill out your story. Let's say you're writing a piece on a recent swine flu death in your town. Is it practical to fly out to Rhode Island to interview the foremost influenza expert for a series of simple quotes and to then jet off to Hawaii to interview a scientist who has published a groundbreaking new study on swine flu? No. (I wish it was, and I would book my flights at the drop of a hat if someone else was footing the bill, but no.)

Even in profiles, you may need quotes from outside sources to pepper your article with third-party perspectives on your subject. Again, it's simply not feasible to fly to four states to interview the source's closest friends.

If you need an expert source from an academic or scientific institution, pick up the phone. If you need a quick quote from a play's artistic director for the theater preview you're writing, pick up the phone. If you need a quote from a politician's campaign manager, pick up the phone.

Phone interviews work best for supplementary items, or for stories about a larger theme that are built on the foundation of small quotes and stories, but they *can* work for bigger articles with heavier focuses. Again, it will just be harder. I've done hundreds, if not thousands, of articles based on phone interviews, and I've probably conducted more phone interviews than any other type. It's just a reality of journalism that you can't be everywhere at once (a fact a writer discovers as he writes for more national outlets).

The key to pulling off a successful article with a phone interview is to make the reader actually believe—and never question—that you were there. It's not trickery or deception—it's good interviewing tactics at their finest, and equally good writing.

THE E-MAIL INTERVIEW

This is where people get opinionated. Teachers and the pros will tell you never do an e-mail interview: Such interviews are lazy, bad journalism, and the purview of bloggers (scandalous, I know).

I have to admit that I tread the old curmudgeonly line on this topic. But I also freely admit that I've done my fair share of them—when I have a story that's ripe for it or calls for it, I will conduct one.

Let's look at the pros and cons of the e-mail interview. We'll start with the arguments of the haters.

E-MAIL INTERVIEWS ARE LAZY. This is, for many journalists, sadly true. After all, it's amazingly easy to blast off a list of questions to a subject, wait a couple of days, and receive the answers in pure text form, no painstaking transcription required. But the problem is, some writers exclusively do this. They've lost all touch with in-person or phone interviews—and don't truly understand their importance.

When an editor finds out that a writer inexplicably conducted all of her interviews for an article via e-mail, he's confounded. *Why would you do that?* It casts doubt on the journalist's abilities and demonstrates a lack of respect for the professionalism required for the job. Had the writer taken the time to do the interviews at least over the phone, she—and by nature, the publication—would probably have gotten a much better story.

E-MAIL INTERVIEWS GIVE YOU ONLY HALF THE STORY. More often than not, this is also true. One of the biggest problems with e-mail interviews is that they kill the interactivity element. How

can you ask a follow-up question if the whole conversation has already happened?

Moreover, if the interview is for a news story, you'll quickly find
that your meatiest questions—especially if they're controversial—have
been quickly breezed over with simple PR responses. You can't press
people in e-mail interviews. (Well, you can, but only through follow-
up—which is rarely ever effective.)

**WHEN YOU DO AN E-MAIL INTERVIEW, YOU'RE GIVING UP
ALL CONTROL.** If you're asking something controversial or digging
into the heart of an issue (be it a news story, a celebrity's debatable
moment, a high-profile legal battle, etc.), there's a very good chance
ten people—PR consultants, bosses, chiefs of communication—will review a subject's responses to make sure they're acceptable. And if they
aren't acceptable, they will edit accordingly, watering down your story.
Think of every thriller film you've ever seen in which a reporter was hot
on the trail of a groundbreaking story and a crucial source broke down
and gave the reporter exactly what she needed in a pivotal, on-the-re-
cord moment. That would not have happened had the director of the
EPA (or whoever) had a chance to minimize his e-mail screen and simply go back to eating lunch. (I should add, too, that Watergate stories
aren't the only pieces affected by this. Public image and public persona
is a very highly controlled and paranoid game, regardless of whether
you're talking to a best-selling author, an actor, a politician, the head of
a local rally, or a shopkeeper.)

YOU RISK GETTING BACK VERY BAD, SHORT ANSWERS.
Most writers have been burned by this. Simply put, you send your
questions off to a source, and he turns in paltry, one-sentence answers.
You're left with a pile of hair on your desk that you pulled out while trying to figure out a way to make the watered-down quotes work in time
to meet your afternoon deadline.

YOU OFTEN END UP ON THE PHONE ANYWAY. The source
didn't respond to you by the deadline and has ignored multiple e-mail
follow-ups? You'll find yourself on the horn with her, asking if she can

fill out the answers—or do a phone interview then and there to meet your deadline.

All of this considered, here are the pros of e-mail interviews:

E-MAIL INTERVIEWS ARE, INDEED, FAST. If you need to interview multiple sources to obtain a few fluffy quotes, this is one way to do it.

SOMETIMES, E-MAIL INTERVIEWS ARE THE ONLY WAY YOU CAN GET THE STORY. Many people are hesitant about talking to journalists and writers, and often for good reason—bad journalists and writers exist in scores, and they've made a chunk of the population afraid to talk to the rest of us. For fear of being misquoted, sounding silly, or any medley of reasons, sources will sometimes refuse to be interviewed unless it's via e-mail. In those situations, it may be the only way you can get the story.

AS MENTIONED, NO TRANSCRIPTION IS NEEDED. If you're in a rush, this can be a lifesaver. Take this example: For the February 2015 issue of *Print* magazine, I had to fill a last-minute gap on the subject of stock photography. The issue was set to go to press in a couple of weeks, which meant I had to find a story, find a subject, interview him or her, write the story, fact-check it, route it among my fellow editors, submit it to my art director for design, approve the design, edit two versions of it on the page, and upload it to production … in roughly fourteen days.

First, I had to find a story with an interesting hook. After doing some digging, I figured out the identity and e-mail address of "the world's most famous model you've never heard of," a stock model whose image had been used in thousands of photos on brands galore. I e-mailed her photographer partner for an interview. He turned me down. I suspect he didn't want the media coverage because identifying her and profiling who she really was would make her, well, less "stock." Fair enough. Four days gone.

Next, I figured I'd write about the history and evolution of stock photography. I dug into the research. There was just too much to root through to do the subject justice in the given time frame. Six days gone.

Next, I received a submission about the subject of stock photography. I considered it. I wished to hell it would work. But it sounded too much like PR. Seven days gone.

Next, I discovered a Danish man named Yuri Arcurs, who was identified as "the world's most famous stock photographer." He had risen to notoriety by selling his work on "microstock" websites. He had made millions in a short time and now had a company employing one hundred people, which seemed like an insurmountable feat—stock photography is not considered the world's most lucrative profession. The question lingered in the air: *How the hell did he do it?* I couldn't find any contact info for him. I logged onto his website, and one of those "How can I help you?" windows popped up. I figured I'd give it a go and explained that I wanted to write about him for my magazine. An agent suggested an e-mail address for one of his assistants. I contacted it. I waited. Ten days gone. I got an e-mail: Yuri would love to do an interview and could do it fast. He was in South Africa. His assistant offered a Skype call on Monday at 11:30 CAT—4:30 A.M. my time. I wrestled with it. I groaned and gritted my teeth and set my alarm. And then I turned the alarm off and e-mailed him the questions instead. I got lucky: He replied quickly, and his responses offered a fascinating look at his profession and meteoric rise. I plopped them into an InDesign template, styled them, and added art from his stock photo collection. It was a solid piece.

But still … I wonder how much better the story would have been if only I had woken up in the wee hours of the morning to chat with him.

E-MAIL INTERVIEWS TRANSCEND TIME ZONES. See above.

E-MAIL INTERVIEWS CAN BE GREAT IF LANGUAGE BARRIERS EXIST. I was working on a story for *National Geographic Kids* about a pod hotel in Japan and was having immeasurable trouble communicating with my source over the phone. The source asked if he could respond via e-mail and noted that he could read and type English better than he could speak it. I reached out to my editor and explained the situation, and she approved it. It saved the day and made for a great story that might not otherwise have been possible without a good translator.

E-MAIL INTERVIEWS CAN BE GOOD FOR QUICK, ONE-OFF Q&AS OR SHORT WEB ARTICLES. I often send Q&As for small stories on *Print*'s website and don't feel the slightest bit of shame doing so.

On the whole, you have to choose the type of interview that pairs best with your article while weighing your time, budget, and resources. I'd love to interview everyone in person, but it's not always possible, so I use the phone. And when the phone isn't possible, I consider booting up my computer.

Let your story—and your inner writerly compass—guide you.

THE REPORTER'S TOOL KIT

Now it's time to get geared up for your interview. For every in-person interview I conduct, I bring the following tool kit (which I've been lugging around since my reporter days):

DIGITAL RECORDER. Journalists get downright superstitious and spiritual about their recorders; I've had a number of Sonys and other brands crap out on me on the job, so I stick by Olympus recorders religiously. My current rig is an Olympus Digital Voice Recorder WS-801,[2] which features dual-stereo microphones, a microSD card slot, a surplus of memory, slo-mo playback, and a built-in USB connector, so I can plug the thing right into the computer and not have to worry about desperately rooting through a labyrinth of lost cords. It's also sturdy and feels as if it wouldn't break into a million plastic slivers if I dropped it.

I recommend that you use a recorder, even if you're a super reporter capable of taking one-to-one real-time notes by hand. As a journalist, you *never* want anyone to accuse you of botching quotes or information. So record everything. Should anyone ever call you to the floor (and I assure you, you don't have to be working on *All the President's Men* for this to happen), you can simply hop onto your computer, pull the file, and assure him that he's been quoted accurately.

Moreover, recording your sources will help you as a writer. I take manual notes when doing interviews, but I often discover revealing or

---

2 This most definitely constitutes an unauthorized endorsement. I promise that if Olympus sends me a fleet of these, I'll distribute them among buyers of this book.

interesting tidbits on my recordings that I may have overlooked during the interview. I frequently comb back through my tapes to search for more info, to fact-check, verify quotes, and deepen stories.

My advice: Don't skimp on a recorder. You can get a good one for less than $100. Often $20 can make the difference between a piece of junk and a more professional-grade device. I go for ones that have a dual mic (useful for recording multiple sources around a table, etc.), a sturdier build, and simple connectivity. Also, choose a recorder that uses universal batteries, such as AA or AAA, so you can easily replace them while you're out and about.

BATTERIES. For the aforementioned easy replacement when I'm out and about, I always carry more than necessary because it's my nightmare to have a recorder go dead during a crucial interview.

NOTEPAD. Again, I take physical notes out of paranoia that a recorder might miss something. (Noticing themes of paranoia here? Remember, writers get esoteric about this stuff.) But I also doodle and pretend to take notes at times to make a source feel comfortable and to avoid awkwardly staring at her the entire time. (More on that in a moment.)

MULTIPLE PENS. The only thing worse than your recorder dying or your pen dying: having to shamefully ask an interviewee for a pen. He'll nervously hand one over, wondering what the hell kind of writer didn't come prepared with the only thing she really needs to do her job.

CELL PHONE. I know some writers who go so far as to bring *two* recorders with them on assignments. While I don't go that far, I make sure that my phone is equipped with a good recording app, should my recorder fail. A cell phone is also good to have on hand in case you're out in the field and receive a call back from a source, and you don't have your recorder on you.

Rich Shivener, who pitched WD the Robert Kirkman Q&A I spotlighted earlier, was set to interview Song of Ice and Fire series author George R.R. Martin for us. Problem was, he'd been having trouble getting in touch with Martin for some crucial follow-up questions to round-out his interview.[3] With a looming deadline, Shivener got a call when he was driving. It was Martin. He pulled over, activated the recording app on his phone, and got what he needed for a great interview.

CAMERA. I've long been an amateur photo nerd, so I carry my Pentax SLR along with me. While you're usually not expected to shoot photos for your story, they make for a nice bonus for an editor—and sometimes, if the art director really likes them, you might even pick up some bonus bucks. That aside, I often shoot photos of a source's home, surroundings, etc. so that I can accurately add detail to fully bring a reader into a scene.

On the whole, more and more editors want journalists who can be jacks-of-all-trades—supplying copy, photos, and sometimes even video for a story. This is where the love/hate term "multimedia journalist" comes into play. Loved by some because you can be that jack-of-all-trades. Hated by others because the writing can often feel less and less like a key part of the equation.

BUSINESS CARDS. It's a tiny gesture, but business cards build your credibility for sources—especially those who might be hesitant to talk to the press. Consider their perspective: You're just an otherwise unknown person with a digital recorder and a bunch of questions. Get some cards, and distribute them liberally. Give one to every person you interview (or approach for an interview). You'd be amazed how great stories will fall into your lap later because a source has a scoop or an idea, and he still has your card from that one time you bumped into him with a question for something you were working on.[4]

LAYING THE FOUNDATION

Now it's time to rope yourself an interview. To show how it's done, let's consider a theoretical article. Let's say you pitched your local newspaper a weekend feature: a profile of a ticket-taker at a prominent Broadway theater in town. He has been taking tickets there for five decades (ever since he was fifteen), loves his job, has a huge personality, and is

---

3 Or, at least, questions I'd deemed crucial and was making the poor guy call Martin back about.

4 Of course, the crazies will also call. Let them! Indulge them! Sometimes the crazies are on to something crazy good.

beloved by theater patrons. You've heard via the grapevine (perhaps from a business card tip!) that his life story is a hell of a tale, and that this year he's celebrating fifty years in the business.

So now that you've gone to the trouble of pitching your story to an editor and it's been commissioned, you must pitch the story to your main source. (When will it end?!)

There are a number of ways you could contact him:

1. **CALL THE THEATER.** Explain who you are and what you're doing: *Hi, my name is Zachary Petit, and I'm working on a story for the* News-Journal. *We heard that Oscar Boynton is celebrating fifty years in the business this year and would love to profile him in the paper. Might you be able to connect us with him?* You'll probably get passed around to a couple of different managers, but at the end of the day, it's good press for the theater, and you'll probably wind up with Boynton's phone number or an invitation to come out to the theater to meet him. From there, all you have to do is get in touch with Boynton, explain the story you'd like to write, and see if he's game.

2. **FIND BOYNTON'S PHONE NUMBER YOURSELF.** You could try Googling, but more often than not, residential phone numbers can be irritatingly difficult to find online thanks to the number of companies trying to charge for access to them. You don't need them cutting into your check. Instead, turn to one of those mystical ten-pound tomes of yesteryear: a White Pages phone book. Despite the "death of print," it miraculously continues to appear on my doorstep, surprising me every time. Pull Boynton's number, and reach out to him directly.

3. **SEND BOYNTON (OR THE THEATER) AN E-MAIL RE-QUESTING AN INTERVIEW.** In this case, since Boynton is a bit older and likely not as obsessed with e-mail as some of us are (read: me)—and because daily newspapers have a tighter turnaround time—this would probably not be the way to go. (But for many stories, it is.)

Your goal here is to make a good first impression, to make Boynton feel comfortable in agreeing to be featured, and to lock down the details so the interview can progress.

Of course, not every interview is as easy of a get as Boynton. So let's take a brief moment to look at the types of sources you may find yourself interviewing—and some ideas for how to best approach them.

YOUR MAIN SUBJECT

In grade school and high school, we're taught about "primary" and "secondary" sources in regard to academic papers. In journalism school, we're taught the same terms—though they mean very different things—when it comes to writing and interviewing human sources. So let's ditch those terms and instead speak like humans: Call the main subject of any article "the main subject" and secondary sources your "secondary sources." Your main subject will be the meat and potatoes of your piece—either the story's focal point, or a central source through which the rest of the story is told.

To reach out to him or her, I usually send a note akin to the following:

> Dear Robert,
>
> I'm a freelance writer for *All Things Science* magazine, a monthly newsstand publication focused on providing deep insight into the latest developments in science and technology (circulation 350,000+).
>
> Recently, your groundbreaking work on particle accelerators has caught our eye, and we'd love to feature you in the magazine.
>
> I work near your offices on 7th Street—would you have any time in the next two weeks, prior to our October 25 deadline, to meet up? Alternatively, if meeting in person is not in the cards in the next couple of weeks, I'd be happy to connect over the phone.
>
> We'd love to share your work with our readers, Robert. Many thanks in advance for your time and consideration.
>
> All my best,
> Zac
> --
>
> Zachary Petit
> Freelance Writer
> [Phone]
> [E-mail]

SECONDARY SOURCES

These are all the people you will use to fill out the rest of the article.
They can be experts, public officials, celebrities, and so on.

For these sources, I usually send a note like this:

> Dear Julia,
>
> I'm a freelance writer for *All Things Science* magazine, a monthly
> newsstand publication focused on providing deep insight into the
> latest developments in science and technology (circulation 350,000+).
>
> Right now we're working on a story about Robert Smith's work
> on particle accelerators. Given your expertise in the field, I'd love to
> be able to ask you a few technical questions and tap your wisdom
> on the subject and Smith's work.
>
> Might you have any time in the next two weeks, prior to our Oc-
> tober 25 deadline, to chat over the phone, since you're currently on
> sabbatical in France?
>
> Many thanks in advance for your time and consideration, Julia.
>
> All my best,
> Zac
> --
> Zachary Petit
> Freelance Writer
> [Phone]
> [E-mail]

Or this one (I bolded the text that differs from the first example):

> Dear Ken,
>
> I'm a freelance writer for *All Things Science* magazine, a monthly
> newsstand publication focused on providing deep insight into the
> latest developments in science and technology (circulation 350,000+).
>
> Right now we're working on a story about Robert Smith's work
> on particle accelerators. **When I spoke with Smith last week, he cit-
> ed you as someone very familiar with his theories and work, and
> suggested I reach out concerning some of the technical elements.**
>
> Might you have any time in the next two weeks, prior to our Oc-
> tober 25 deadline, to have a brief chat over the phone?
>
> Many thanks in advance for your time and consideration, Julia.[5]

---

5 When copying and pasting e-mails to send to sources, always double-check
that you've subbed in the correct names!

All my best,
Zac
--
Zachary Petit
Freelance Writer
[Phone]
[E-mail]

Here are the takeaways for these sample e-mails:

- Clearly identify who you are, and your capacity as a freelance writer. Never misrepresent yourself as an actual staffer of a publication—editors get touchy about that.
- Offer a bit of background about the publication. Even though your sources may very well know of your outlet, it's always good to remind them—especially when you can throw in a tasty circulation figure about how big the publication's reach is, allowing them insight into the benefit of being interviewed by you.
- Offer some brief background about what you want to write, but don't give too much detail. You never know when the scope of the interview or subsequent article could change: The magazine's publishing schedule could shift, a bad interview for a feature article could get cut down to a sidebar, and so on. Also, unless the editor explicitly states that this piece will run as the cover story, don't promise this to the interviewee. That's a tactic often used to get a big-name source to agree to an interview, but you should only deploy it when it's an absolute certainty.
- Don't be afraid to lightly flatter the interviewee if the situation merits it, especially if the source is a big-name subject whom you're planning to portray in a solid, objective light.
- Specifically state *when* you'd like the interview to take place and mention the deadline so the subject knows to answer the request promptly.
- Include your phone number and e-mail address so the source can utilize the one she's most comfortable with.

ACCESS HOLLYWOOD

But what if you need/want to interview a famous person?

If you don't have an "in" or a personal connection, or if a PR person hasn't reached out to you offering an interview, there are some standard operating procedures you can put into action.

In general, anyone deemed a "celebrity" will have a set of gatekeepers and handlers. (And sometimes, comically, even those significantly below that level will, too.) Your mission is to find these handlers and contact them directly to pitch the article you have in mind.

Say you want to interview *Fight Club* author Chuck Palahniuk for a pop-culture magazine. You'd start with a simple Google search for "Chuck Palahniuk." It will bring up Palahniuk's website. First, go for the Hail Mary and try to find his direct e-mail address on the site.

Surprise, surprise—it's not listed.

Your next step: Take your Google search up a notch. Google "Chuck Palahniuk agent." Palahniuk's agency's website, Donadio & Olson, will be your first hit, and it will list his agent there.

But let's say it isn't so simple. Let's say nothing but junk comes up. Your next step is to see if any databases might be able to help out. AgentQuery.com is a great, simple, and free database of literary agents. If you hop over there and enter an author's name, it will bring up the author's agent and list his or her contact details.

If you still haven't had any luck, pop open one of the author's books. Turn to the acknowledgments. More often than not, the author will thank his agent.

From there, you can draft a simple e-mail:

> Dear Edward,
> I hope all is well your way. I'm a freelance writer for *All Things Pop* magazine, a monthly newsstand publication focused on pop culture, writers, film, and all things related (circulation 50,000+).
> Right now we're naming our top ten most impactful pop writers of the decade, and we'd love to feature Chuck Palahniuk on the list. Might you be able to gauge his interest in an interview with us?

We're working off a September 2 deadline and would love it if Chuck would be able to connect in person or over the phone prior to that date.

Many thanks in advance for your time and consideration, Edward.

All my best,
Zac

--

Zachary Petit
Freelance Writer
[Phone]
[E-mail]

Agents are busy people. Among their many other responsibilities, they are often totally inundated with media requests. Don't be upset if you don't receive an immediate response. Contact them well in advance of your deadline, and send reasonably timed follow-ups.

Moreover, understand that the agent is sometimes not even the appropriate contact. Celebrities often have multiple sets of handlers. Some strictly handle contracts. Others happily field media requests. Others may be annoyed that you reached out to them and will forward you to the publicity department of the subject's latest project.

Which brings up an alternate tactic: Track down the appropriate publicist or the publicity department's general e-mail. For an author, it would be the publisher. A simple Google search of the author's publisher plus "media contacts" or "publicity department" should send you in the right direction.

But what if you were feeling masochistic and wanted to interview, say, Miley Cyrus?

Seems like a long shot, no?

I've never interviewed Miley Cyrus, nor have I tried. So I'm going to conduct a real-time experiment to try to track down the best contact for her.

… and five minutes later, I'm back.

As of this writing, if I were going to try to interview Miley, I'd start with Meghan Prophet: meghan.prophet@pmkbnc.com.

Here's how I came to that conclusion.

A search of "Miley Cyrus agent" tosses you straight into the problematic thicket of big celebs: They have agents galore, from acting to literary. Moreover, insane amounts of websites and promotion companies pop up with things like "Contact Miley now!" and a slew of hopeless resources and names lacking consistency. In other words, rabbit holes and wastes of time. (However, I lost a good solid minute reading a gossipy Fox News article about whether or not Cyrus's publicists were responsible for her transformation from child star to sex symbol.)

So I closed that tab and began anew with "Miley Cyrus publicist."

Some light Googling brings up a slew of reputable news articles quoting Meghan Prophet as Miley's publicist.

The game is afoot!

A search for Prophet brings up the name PMK*BNC, a massive Hollywood talent PR firm. A good sign.

A search for "Meghan Prophet PMKBNC" brings up a set of press releases from 2011 and 2013 regarding Miley in which Prophet is cited as the appropriate PR contact. It includes her e-mail address.

But is she still Cyrus's current PR contact?

A search of "Meghan Prophet Miley Cyrus" brings up a news story from a few weeks ago about Miley having an allergic reaction to antibiotics. And there is Prophet, telling the press that everything is going to be okay.

So is she still at PMK*BNC? A further search of "Meghan Prophet PMKBNC" brings up a *Variety* page listing her as the VP of talent. Further searches corroborate her as still being at PMK*BNC.

While I didn't dare take this grave experiment any further, if I had to contact Miley, that's where I'd start.

So, what are your chances of actually roping a big fish?

It depends on a vast variety of factors. Obviously the higher you go up the food chain, the more difficult access becomes. Sure, *People* magazine has a Rolodex of celebrity contacts, and no doubt Miley is in there. But that doesn't improve your chances as a freelancer pitching a story.

You want to play up the publication you're pitching it for. You want to offer any connections you can find between the celeb and that publication. (Did Miley once say she was obsessed with *All Things Pop*? Did she once compliment something you wrote on Twitter? Now's the time to deploy those secret weapons.) You want to explain the unique angle you're offering and why it's a great fit for the celeb so her publicist can begin to see the merit in going to the trouble of setting it up.

Time plays a factor (publicists will respond very differently to a request for a ten-minute interview than a four-hour one). Current projects play a factor. (If Miley has a new movie coming out and an impending press tour scheduled, or if her new clothing line is launching, this could affect the response positively.) Luck plays a huge factor.

But there's a whole other layer of difficulty in addition to getting in touch with Miley. If you want to write a story about a celeb or other notable source, you face the conundrum of whether you should pitch the idea to the publication or the celebrity first.

Your pitch to the publication will carry extra weight if you've already gotten confirmation that the celebrity is interested. But your pitch to the celebrity will carry extra weight if you have a great publication on board, ready to run the story.

So how do you choose?

It's a tough question. As an editor, I've accepted both types of queries. But I'll admit, I'm more drawn into a query if it mentions a brief preliminary sign of interest from the source, even if it's vague. Again, editors are afraid of commissioning a story, reserving a spot for it, and then coming up short on page counts because something fell through. The more reassurance you can give, the better.

A NOTE ON TAPE RECORDING (AND NOT GETTING SUED)

Now that we've gotten our interviews locked down, this would be a good time to deploy a heavy-duty disclaimer about recording. None of us wants to end up in jail.

The government decided to confuse all of us writers by allowing individual states to determine the laws about who needs to be aware that you're recording. In many states, you need only one-party consent—in other words, you, the writer, would be the only person who needs to know that the recorder is on. In other states, *all*—not just both, *all*—parties need to know that the recorder is on.

This should not be cause for stress or concern, assuming you're not setting up any Watergate bugs. Regardless of which state I'm in, to cover myself, I simply set the recorder on the table once we get going and casually ask if it's okay if I record the interview so I can refer back to quotes, check my notes, and so on. The sources are usually relieved to hear that—not only does it take away the "gotcha!" element that often maligns journalists wielding recorders, but it also shows the source that you care about accuracy and precision. Being misquoted is one of the biggest fears and complaints of celebrities and others, but you can't be misquoted if it's being recorded. (And should anyone ever accuse you of misquoting them, you'll be able to prove that you didn't.)

Of course, you may find yourself in a scenario in which your recorder is rolling in your pocket because you're reporting on an investigative story and you catch wind of something big. It doesn't just happen in cloak-and-dagger movies, either—I've been there myself. And in those instances, you sure as hell better bet that I knew whether or not I could legally record what was unfolding.

Below is a quick overview of the laws as of the writing of this book. For the most up-to-date information and a deeper look at the fine print, I highly recommend Reporters Committee for Freedom of the Press (rcfp.org), which also recaps the laws for video recording, etc.

- **LOCALES WHERE ONLY YOU NEED TO KNOW THE RECORDER IS RUNNING:** Alabama, Alaska, Arizona, Arkansas, Colorado, Delaware, District of Columbia, Georgia, Hawaii, Idaho, Indiana, Iowa, Kansas, Kentucky, Louisiana, Maine, Minnesota, Mississippi, Missouri, Nebraska, New Jersey, New Mexico, New York, North Carolina, North Dakota, Ohio, Oklahoma, Oregon, Rhode Island, South Carolina, South Dakota, Tennessee, Texas, Utah, Vermont, Virginia, West Virginia, Wisconsin, Wyoming
- **LOCALES WHERE *ALL* PARTIES MUST KNOW THE RECORDER IS RUNNING:** California, Connecticut, Florida, Illinois, Maryland, Massachusetts, Michigan, Montana, Nevada, New Hampshire, Pennsylvania, Washington (state)

POPPING THE QUESTIONS

Now that our legal defenses have been mounted, let's tackle the next part of the pre-interview process: drafting some questions.

Every writer has her own system for drafting and subsequently deploying questions. Some come up with questions beforehand and stick meticulously close to the script. Others draft their questions but ditch them once the interview is underway and the conversation takes on a life of its own. Others don't write any at all.

I wish I could say I was one of those writers who acts on pure instinct and inner wisdom and doesn't utilize prefabricated questions, but I'm not. Instead, I come up with a well-thought-out list beforehand and flag the most important ones so that even if the conversation takes a turn, I can make sure to get my biggies answered and my story delivered in the way the editor wants.

The nature of your questions will depend on how well known your subject is and the angle of your piece.

Let's return to Old Man Boynton, the theater ticket-taker who will be celebrating fifty years in the business this year. Nobody has written about him before, so you have a blank canvas to work from (always a delight). But on the downside, you can't dig up any research on him, so it's all up to you and this interview.

When drafting questions, I start by letting my mind go wild with curiosity. I push the fact that I'm writing an article out of my head and do some free-form musing, furiously scribbling as I go. Just let it all fall onto the page. You can organize and sharpen it all later.

For Boynton, I might come up with a list like this:

- What year were you born?
- Where were you born?
- What were your parents like?
- What was your childhood like?
- What did you like to do to pass the time?
- When did you go to the theater for the first time?
- What did you think while walking into the theater for the first time?
- What drew you to the theater?

- When you first started working there, what were you doing?
- How was the theater different then compared to now?
- Did you ever think when you started that you'd be there this long?
- *Why* did you stay this long?
- What have been some of your favorite shows that have come through the theater? Why? Which have been most memorable?
- What are some of your most memorable moments at the theater?
- What's the strangest thing you've witnessed?
- Funniest?
- Saddest?
- How has the theater fared over the years? Were there a lot of ups and downs?
- How would you characterize its vitality now, given your decades of experience?
- Do you see all the shows?
- How many do you estimate you've seen?
- What happens after you take the tickets for a show? What else goes on behind the scenes that patrons would be surprised about?
- Are you married?
- Do you have kids? If so, what do they think about the theater and you working here for so long?
- Ever hope your kids will get into the business, too?
- You're known by patrons as an institution. How does that make you feel?
- What do you hope your legacy is?
- How long do you want to keep doing it?
- Think you'll ever retire?
- What's your best advice to the next ticket-taker? Seems like he or she will have big shoes to fill.
- Who has meant the most to you during your time working here?

And so on.

Your goal with these questions is to plant seeds during the course of your conversation with Boynton so that different elements will blossom into personal stories, narrative, character, context, and anecdotes readers will eat up, and the necessary details to fill out the bones of your story. Simply put, your goal is to get him talking. You can then interact and respond, fleshing things out as you go, and changing direction when needed.

At this stage in the drafting process, I organize the questions and try to build a chronological flow so that when I actually ask them during the interview, they take on the natural cadence of a conversation while still supplying me with crucial information. Using this approach, the source will answer many of your questions before you ask them.

Once I feel I have a good skeleton, I then think: *What's missing? What am I overlooking? What do I need to ask now so that I don't have to harass him later with follow-ups? Is there an opportunity to elicit a telling detail that I'm overlooking?*

When I'm confident the questions cover all the practical bases while providing opportunities for him to convey his personality and potentially even some humor ("What's your best advice to the next ticket-taker?" feels like it could lead to a great closing line for the article), I'll go through and identify my must-haves. I bold these throughout the list. In this case, I'd probably bold:

- **When did you go to the theater for the first time?**
- **Did you ever think when you started that you'd be there this long?**
- **What are some of your most memorable moments at the theater?**
- **What happens after you take the tickets for a show? What else goes on behind the scenes that patrons would be surprised about?**
- **What do you hope your legacy is?**

Why bold these must-haves? I do so because in the event our interview gets cut short, or we get on a serious tangent, I can make sure that, come hell or high water, I get answers to the essentials needed for the piece. My bolded list will provide some great scene-setting details and stories that could work as narrative.

Once I have everything organized, I cut. Having too many questions will not only clutter your interview, but you'll also be shuffling endless pages like those blue cards James Lipton is always combing through. While celebrities may enjoy such things, real people get horrified and distracted by the *War and Peace*-sized list you're trying to conceal on your lap.

Once I've killed all my darlings, I print out the list.

And then it's time to dance, Old Man Boynton.

THE IN-PERSON INTERVIEW

Let's go step-by-step through best practices for each type of interview, starting with the in-person. Say you dropped by the theater, as scheduled, and began your process by observing as Boynton takes tickets to get a feel for him and how he interacts with patrons.

Even before you begin the formal interview, take notes. Jot down what he's saying to people. Little quips he might offer up. Patrons who call him by name. Note what he's wearing, the color of his shoes, what type of jewelry he has on, how tall he is, his hair color, what he's drinking—all details, and some telling details, that can help you set a scene, should you want to. You are not waiting on him to finish so you can interview him. You're watching him in his true environment, in action.

After everyone is seated and his work is done, it's time to go to a meeting room behind-the-scenes for your interview.

1. MAKE HIM COMFORTABLE. First, get the basics out of the way and set the stage for a good conversation. If you haven't already, shake his hand, introduce yourself, and thank him for his time. Explain who you're working for and what the publication is, what sort of story you're working on, and why you want to write about him. Many sources, as mentioned earlier, are afraid of journalists and are paranoid about saying the wrong thing or being burned. For that reason, I stay professional yet personable, putting the source at ease that I'm not out to get him or unfairly represent him.

Make a positive first impression. Your goal here is to make him comfortable. If he's uncomfortable, there's a good chance you'll walk away with a bad interview.

I also tend to adjust my personality to the tone and approach of the person I'm interviewing. If he's deathly serious, I tend to be, too, within reason. If he's joking and personable, I let that side of myself show. I reflect whatever kind of personality or tone they're exhibiting to a certain degree, and in doing so, they tend to be comfortable talking to me.

2. GET A FEEL FOR THE SOURCE, AND BE CONSCIOUS OF YOUR TIME. When you begin interacting with your source, you'll immediately get a sense of how the interview is going to go. I usually ask a few icebreaker questions right off the bat, not only to make the interaction feel more normal but also to test the waters. When you say, "So, how's your day going so far?" you will hear any number of responses that will clue you in. "Fine," with no follow-up, means that you need to keep chipping away at the wall, or that you're dealing with a very guarded source. On the opposite end of the spectrum, if a source launches into a fifteen-minute aside, you're dealing with a different problem—an interview you'll likely be battling to control. This is why I bold questions on my question sheet—when I only have the source for thirty minutes, and it becomes apparent that he's going to talk about all kinds of things, I know which core questions I have to hit and can steer the interview in a way that I can interject the questions naturally.

3. BREAK OUT THE RECORDER. I usually keep it out of sight for a moment so it doesn't set an awkward tone for the conversation. Eventually, as we talk more and begin to approach the questions, I'll casually bring it out and ask, almost as an aside, if it's okay to record the conversation to ensure all quotes are accurate. This is not trickery but rather a means of putting the source further at ease. I keep the questions unobtrusively in my lap for the same reason. I don't want the source to feel that he's about to be grilled or for him to see the long list and feel as if he's going to be incessantly bombarded for the next thirty minutes to an hour.

4. GET TO IT. When you see a natural transition to the beginning of the interview, casually dive in. I wait until all the introductory elements are out of the way, and then when we have that natural "Well, let's get to it" pause, I'll just say, "Is it okay if I dive into the first question?" The first questions are generally background questions, so they're softballs. They set the course to move toward the more involved—and, sometimes, awkward—questions.

5. LET THE INTERVIEW DEFINE ITS OWN FLOW. After a few years of trying to be the master of interviews, set the pace, and closely adhere to the script, I realized that it's not always the best way to go—and that giving up a certain amount of control results in a better story. For example, rather than going down the list and being irritated when a source begins to pursue an aside, let the source run with the aside for a moment. Often it will lead toward something unexpected—and great—that might just make your story. Remember, your source is the story, and there's no way you could know him intimately enough to anticipate everything he's going to say. Let the leash out and let him roam. (But if things start to get out of hand, gently bring him back on topic.)

An interview should be a *conversation*. Give up some control and converse, and see where things go. This is especially vital in a piece that will run as a straight Q&A. When I read old Q&As I did in my early years as a writer, they feel wooden and false. A great thought spoken by a source will be followed up by a question from me that is completely disconnected and unrelated to that thought, and it kills the flow of a piece. Had I asked for more detail on what the source had just said rather than checking off questions from a list in the order I wrote them, the piece would have felt much more natural, organic, and unified.

To remedy this, I reread my questions thoroughly before beginning an interview so that they're lurking in my subconscious, and I can often interject key questions naturally to tie into what the source is saying.

6. OBSERVE AND REPORT. Remember to not lose yourself so completely in the conversation or in jotting down quotes that you neglect to study your source on the scene. I make a number of observations as we're talking, such as "soft voice, soft-spoken," or "eyes wide at 3:34" or "nervous at first, reserved" or "booming voice." All of these things can be used later to tune up a story or give it some life.

7. STAY UP TO DATE. While I warned against mowing through your questions start to finish and calling it a day, I do cross off questions as I go through them. When a source finishes what he's saying and looks at you, signaling he's ready for the next question, you don't want to awkwardly mumble an apology as you flip through pages of questions, trying to figure out where you were—and maybe, just maybe, planting the seed in your source's head that you're not as qualified as he thought.

8. AGAIN, KEEP AN EYE ON THAT CLOCK. You don't want to walk out of the room with half the story. If Old Man Boynton really starts ramblin', go back to the script.

9. SAY WHAT? As you're going along, if something doesn't add up or make sense, interject and ask for clarity. A simple "Can you explain that just a bit more?" will save you a follow-up call later, should you wind up back at your desk with a great line that you'd like to include that needs some more context or explanation.

10. SAVE THE HARDBALLS FOR THE MIDDLE TO END OF THE INTERVIEW. This is a classic journalistic tactic but a vital one. Simply put, you don't want to start your interview on the wrong foot with a question that will both alienate and upset your source. In that case, rapport immediately dies. Rather, you want to cover some basics first. Again, the strategy here is not deception. If your source senses through your earlier questions that you're an ethical journalist wanting to portray the *whole* story and are interested in more than controversy, he'll be more likely to discuss sticky topics down the line.

11. RECAP. As things are winding down, take stock of your question list again. Is there anything that you absolutely must get in before time is up?

12. DON'T FORGET THE FINAL QUESTION. In every interview, I ask this at the very end: "Is there anything we haven't discussed so far that you think is important to add?" A source may say, "Nope"—but not all of them do. You'd be surprised about the quality of information you can get from lobbing the ball midcourt as the buzzer tolls, simply because you asked.

THE PHONE INTERVIEW

Bad news. The day before your interview, you get a call from Boynton. Apparently, in addition to being a theater staple, he's also a weekend warrior outdoorsman. Which is both good—hey, this gives you an extra layer for the story and a further dimension on an already fascinating subject—and bad. A rattlesnake bit Boynton. He was transported to a hospital in the next state to recuperate under the knowing eye of the foremost snake-bite doctor in the country. (Come on, it could happen.)

You won't be able to interview him at the theater tomorrow. But the good news is that he wants to be featured and doesn't want to leave you hanging, so he'll reserve some time to speak by phone tomorrow, in between his antivenom sessions and post-traumatic snake disorder therapy.

The game has changed. But that doesn't mean you should throw the in-person interview tips completely out the window. *Play by the same best practices you'd use at an in-person interview.* Just because you're phoning your source doesn't mean you should phone in the interview. In fact, in-person and phone interviews have much in common. What follows here are tips exclusive to phone interviews. Here's how you can make the best of the situation, rattlesnakes be damned.

1. GET PREPARED. Channel your inner Boy Scout. Just like with my recorders, I plan everything for a phone interview according to Murphy's Law. I fully anticipate my computer crashing because a squirrel outside chews through the right cord at the right time or a fly ball at a Little League game dings the cell phone tower and drops my call, and I make everything as foolproof as possible. I print out all of my questions even though they're on my screen. I don't want to sheepishly explain to an editor how the story is late because I *knew* I should have run all those squirrels off years ago when they started congregating on the power lines outside my house.

2. BE SOMEWHERE QUIET. Live next to a railroad or a subway platform? Get out of the house. Have a pack of hungry kids playing in the next room? Relocate. Have dogs in your house? I have three. Once, I was conducting an interview with a source in the Netherlands who had a thick accent, and the mailman came. My recording of that conversation suddenly erupts into a series of barks, whimpers, and shrieks of joy and resentment, ensuring that the last thing I would ever hear on the tape is a quote in a Dutch accent. Now, if it's a nice day, the dogs play in the backyard while Daddy works.

3. STAY IN ONE LOCATION—AND MAKE SURE IT HAS RELIA-BLE PHONE SERVICE. If you're in the car and pass through a tunnel, you may miss the best quote of your life. (You'll never know.)

4. KNOW YOUR SOURCE'S LOCATION. Time zones and the availability of your source are obvious considerations. But you don't want to realize at the last minute that the number you're calling is an international number, which, depending on the location, your phone plan, and the time of the call, may make the conversation so expensive that the bill outweighs your paycheck. For international calls, I use the Skype app on my cell phone. The clarity of the call and the service work reliably, and you can buy credit online for pennies on the dollar you would pay a telephone provider.

5. FIGURE OUT THE BEST WAY TO RECORD. If I'm at my magazine's office, I use the company's landlines. You can buy an inexpensive adapter at RadioShack[6] that you plug directly into the phone and then into your recorder. If I'm working from my home office, I use my cell phone. Rather than using an in-phone recorder, as some of my colleagues do, I simply put my phone on speaker and set the recorder directly next to the speakers. Once everything is rigged up, have a friend or colleague make a test call to ensure all is working properly. As an editor, I've had writers experience horror stories in which their device didn't work properly or was on the wrong setting, or the adapter was plugged into the earpiece jack rather than the microphone jack—which is one of the easiest (and most traumatic) ways to make sure only one end of the call is recorded.

6. IF YOU'RE GOING TO RECORD, LET YOUR SOURCE KNOW YOU'RE GOING TO DO SO IN THE GENTLE MANNER DE-SCRIBED EARLIER. As we know, recording laws vary by state. Including your disclaimer in every phone interview ensures that regardless of where your source is at the moment, you'll be covered should she call you out later. (It's a long shot, but always a possibility.)

---

6 Assuming it still exists when this book publishes. Turns out people aren't headed to strip malls in droves for radios and weird cords these days.

7. AS SOON AS YOU START, GET YOUR SOURCE'S DIGITS IF YOU DON'T HAVE THEM. This happens when a source calls you, or calls from a line that doesn't include her direct extension in caller ID, which is common in big companies. If you have her number, you can call her back easily should you lose the connection.

8. ARTICULATE. SPEAK CLEARLY. BE CONSCIOUS OF YOUR VOICE (BUT NOT PARANOID ABOUT IT). Good, clear communication is key. Moreover, your voice is your only representative in a phone interview. Present it as you would like to be perceived.

9. REALIZE THAT SILENCE IS YOUR FRIEND. This is important during in-person interviews but often more effective in phone interviews, where all you have is the audio. Don't shy away from awkward pauses. Rather, embrace silence. You may hate it, but your source does, too. If you ask a question and there's silence, wait it out. The response you receive can often be the best part of the interview or the nugget of truth you were seeking. Zen teachings are right: Silence is the path to enlightenment.

10. DON'T BE TIMID IF THE INTERVIEW GETS OUT OF HAND. If your source goes on an epic tangent or the interview derails badly, it can be harder to retake the reins on the phone. Contrary to an in-person interview, you can't just hold up your hand as an interjection or make one of those "I'm beginning to speak" faces that can pause a conversation. Rather, if things are starting to totter on the rails, wait for a natural pause, interrupt, apologize, and set things on the right path so you can walk away from the interview with what you need to write a great story.

11. OBSERVE AND REPORT, PHONE EDITION. Remember when I said to jot down details (and seek the telling detail) during in-person interviews? Do the same for phone interviews. In my transcripts, I note pauses, hesitations, laughter, scoffing, groaning, and everything else that makes the conversation human. I sometimes use them in stories.

> When I ask Boynton why he has been doing this so long, he laughs. "Probably because theater patrons don't tend to bring rattlesnakes in," he says.

Or in a Q&A:

PETIT: Why have you been doing this so long?

BOYNTON: [laughs] Probably because theater patrons don't tend to bring rattlesnakes in.

Note the details, and also try to intuit as much as you can from a source based on her demeanor and reactions in a phone interview. You may walk away with little insight into the person, but sometimes you walk away with a great deal. There are clues in every response, every pause, every quick breath, about who someone really is. You just need to learn to read her.

12. DON'T FORGET TO CONVERSE. This is the essence of the form—and what you lose when you do an interview using e-mail. Use conversation to its fullest. Just because you're on the phone doesn't mean you're not having a human interaction.

THE E-MAIL INTERVIEW

Even worse news. Boynton's condition following the rattlesnake attack is far grimmer than initially thought. He was bitten by a rare, media-wary rattlesnake, and the snake's venom has rendered poor Boynton temporarily mute. (Don't worry, though; Boynton's team of experts believes he'll be back to taking tickets in two months, and the community has rallied to pay his medical bills and to begin an awareness campaign about the nefarious speech-stealing snakes.) You explained to your editor the necessity of conducting the interview via e-mail and she approved, as long as the responses he sends are good. So you pop open your browser, momentarily pause to listen for rattles, and begin to compose. Because you won't have any chance to interact with your source, the hard work of successfully doing an e-mail interview is in carefully crafting your questions.

1. BE PROFESSIONAL, AND SET A GOOD TONE. Begin your e-mail by quickly recapping who you are, the publication you're writing for, and what the story is about. Thank your source for taking the time to do it. Then forget the small talk that would accompany an in-person or phone interview, and jump right in.

2. BE STRATEGIC. Much like a Q&A-style piece, in an e-mail interview, you need to make sure your questions are as refined and clear as possible. Is anything in the questions confusing? Smooth it out, because if a source doesn't understand it, you'll either get an off-base response or he'll skip it. Also make sure your questions have a logical narrative flow and all the other good traits we discussed previously.

3. BE EVEN MORE STRATEGIC. This is a must for any type of interview, but particularly for e-mail interviews: Ask open-ended questions. In an in-person interview, asking "Do you like working here?" might net you a single-word answer, but you could easily follow up with "Why?" Since you don't have that luxury in an e-mail interview, I would simply phrase the question "Do you like working here—and why?" You want to leave room for as much extrapolation and detail as possible.

4. BEFORE SENDING THE Q&A TO YOUR SOURCE, EDIT MERCILESSLY. To me, this is always the hardest part to balance. My biggest fear in e-mail interviews is having to send a slew of follow-ups and wait for responses. My second biggest fear is including a "kitchen-sink"–style list of questions that frightens the source or causes a significant delay in his response. One result of question bloat is that a source, realizing that he has a long road ahead of him, will offer only a few words in response to each inquiry. In an in-person or phone interview, it doesn't matter if my questions are a mile long. I can choose to skip them or kill them in real time. Not so in the e-mail interview. Read and reread your questions several times over. Can any be consolidated? Can others be cut? It's going to be painful, but you need to kill your darlings to keep things manageable for your source. Sharpen your questions list to the very best and most essential.

5. SET A DEADLINE. Explicitly state a reasonable date to get the responses back. And ask if it is doable—doing so prompts action on the source's part and lessens the chance that he might overlook it. A simple "We're hoping to have our story wrapped up by the end of September. Would a deadline of September 19 be doable?" Remember: The further out you work, the more wiggle room you'll have and the more time you'll be able to give your source to answer the questions. For a magazine story, I ideally like to give my source about a week. Any shorter and he may feel too pressured. Any longer and he may sit on the questions and/or forget about them.

6. DON'T BE AFRAID TO SET OTHER PARAMETERS. For one story, I may be paranoid about getting only single-word answers to questions. For another, I may have limited space for the Q&A. For that reason I'll include a note to the source such as "Feel free to dive into each question in as much detail as you would like. Our philosophy is the more, the better." Or "We're hoping for just a sentence or two in response to each question."

7. CROSS YOUR FINGERS. Perhaps the penultimate reason most writers knock e-mail interviews is because they're truly at the mercy of their source, and an e-mail interview is a Hail Mary—you may get great responses, or you may get thirty unusable words in response to twenty well-thought-out questions. If that does happen, shoot the source a note thanking him for taking the time to do it—and noting that you have a few follow-ups. Would the source be up for a quick call to knock them out?

OFF-THE-RECORD SOURCES

Like e-mail interviews, on-spec writing, and, well, I suppose, *most* topics in writing, there are different schools of thought on off-the-record conversations. Throughout my career, I've observed that most journalists have a personal code when it comes to the topic.

As an overview, let's oversimplify a wildly complex subject and look at it through two lenses. First, some journalists have a flat policy that there is no "off the record." It doesn't exist. When you're talking to a journalist, you're talking to a journalist, and anything is fair game.

Conversely, the second school of thought embraces off-the-record discussions to deepen their investigations, further their knowledge of a subject, and so on.

While the first approach would make life easier, I'm of the second school. To me, an interview is a game of trust and balance. If a source can't trust you, you're not going to get the whole story. It's psychology. If a source wants to give me a deep insight into something she's discussing but is not comfortable revealing to the public at large—often it's something that is personal or something that will lead me to the truth—and asks me if she can speak to me candidly off the record, I'll let her. Of course, I don't advertise that I'm of this school of thought, and I don't welcome it when it happens. (I'd rather not have to deal with it, and to have all information and insight happily volunteered to me, but that's not the way the world always works.) If what she's said to me is something I believe should be on the record for the betterment of the pursuit of the truth or the story, I'll attempt to convince her to say it on the record.

Whenever anyone goes off the record, you should immediately question *why* she's doing so. Was it so she could let you know that she's uncomfortable discussing the disease you've asked her about because her husband died of the same terrible illness a year ago? Fair enough. If it's personal information unrelated to the greater story, I would accept that and change topics. But if it's a telling detail of crucial importance to understanding the subject at hand, I'd let the source know that and express why I think she should be willing to say it on the record.

But let's say you're interviewing a local mayoral candidate, and she asks to go off the record and then tells you that her opponent has an underground lemur fighting ring. *Why* is she telling you this?

Politicians love to play with reporters—and play reporters. They know if they give you a scoop like that, it will hurt their opponent.

So you look into it. If it's true and you have verified it without a doubt, yes, it would be newsworthy and worth pursuing. But if you look into it, you might just discover that it's a pointless smear campaign based on the fact that the candidate once owned an exotic pet lemur two decades ago. His lemur cage matches are distorted fantasies from the other side.

People have reasons galore for wanting to manipulate writers. It's your job to fight the good fight, look into every fact presented to you, and vet those facts as a professional. If we write about something that isn't true, we're failing at our jobs—and contributing both to stereotypes about the media and unfortunate *facts* about the media.[7]

We must be responsible.

---

7 By the way, have you watched *The Newsroom* on HBO? Genoa!

I will never burn someone by reporting something she told me off the record. Similarly, I hope to never be misled into reporting something that isn't the whole truth.

What you do with off-the-record info is all about choosing wisely and carefully. But I'm willing to take the plunge and let sources speak to me off the record to see which choice I have to make.

If you take the majority of the biggest news stories that have been broken by writers in the last century, I guarantee you that all of them had an off-the-record source who either leaked a story to a writer or merely pointed him in the right direction.

THE ANONYMOUS SOURCE

And now our discussion bleeds into even murkier waters: working with the anonymous source.

This is where I tend to draw the line. The anonymous source is essentially someone who doesn't want to be identified at all but wants to speak on the record under the veil of, well, anonymity.

Journalists contend that the public looks down on anonymous sources because they hurt a media outlet's trust factor. Truth be told—and this is going to sound arrogant, but I speak honestly from the ground, absent of any high horses—I don't think the public knows enough about news theory to care. People today are reared on the culture of TMZ.

Rather, journalists' real issue with anonymous sources is their knowledge of what can go *wrong* and the problems anonymous sources have historically caused. Consider *why* the source wants to be anonymous. Does he have a good reason? Yes, if a source's life or livelihood could be jeapordized by blowing a whistle, he may be a candidate for anonymity. If the source has committed a crime, he would also not want to incriminate himself. But I've never run into these circumstances, so I've never granted anonymity in an interview. When I've considered it, I've always been able to find someone else willing to go on the record about whatever Deep Throat was telling me.

Interviewing anonymous sources can go terribly awry: These sources may be working to derail a certain cause or defame a certain person. They can also simply be made up by a writer and dropped into an article to make it work. (I recommend the film *Shattered Glass*, the fascinating true story and perhaps cautionary tale of Stephen Glass, the great fabricator at *The New Republic* who invented his own cast of characters.)

But all of this isn't to say I wouldn't grant anonymity, given the right set of circumstances, and if a story couldn't be told without the anonymous source. But if you do want to run an anonymous source, be prepared: An editor will likely want to know the name and can refuse to run a piece unless you give it. Think of it not as needless opposition to your piece but a necessary system of checks and balances.

In our industry, we need them.[8]

DIFFICULT SOURCES

If you ask writers who have been in the game for any length of time about problem sources, we'll all roll up our sleeves and show you a collection of gnarly cat scratches, fading lacerations, and old bullet wounds. Problem sources are those whose very presence can derail a story and make you wish you'd never taken it on in the first place. They come in all shapes and sizes, and the more you work on stories and the deeper your intuition grows, you begin to develop a barometer to spot them a mile away. (In most cases, anyway. Every so often, one of them will steal upon you in the night and abduct your article.)

---

[8] I was originally going to include a chapter in this book about ethics but soon came to the conclusion that the subject is worthy of a book of its own. To include a pithy chapter here would do the subject—and you—a great disservice. There are numerous great writing/reporting ethics books out there. I recommend that every writer read one (or several). They offer not only philosophical advice but also historical examples of media ethics gone awry. On a similar note, I'm sometimes asked if attending journalism school is actually worth the time and money. My answer is that, from a practical standpoint, you can't really learn anything about the job until you actually have a chance to do it. But I add that journalism school *is* worth it for the ethics classes and historical grounding. My ethical standpoint, in a nutshell: Don't be a shitty person. Don't give journalists a bad name. We already have one. Therefore, it's our mission to be the journalists, every day, who surprise their sources by making them realize we are good people and good storytellers who adhere to the facts and are guided by a strong moral compass. Do what you need to do to accomplish that, and you'll be on your way. Or, as my teacher Charles St. Cyr once wrote to me, framing the subject in a much more succinct and eloquent way: "Ethics is most notable in its absence. ... Remember: We are mere mortals, no matter how much we may romanticize what journalism can be. The bottom line always is the same: Can you live with yourself?"

Here are a few of the usual suspects—and how you might deal with them, should you cross paths.

THE OFF-THE-RECORD-PRONE SOURCE

This seems like a good place to start, given the paragraphs that led us here. As I mentioned, I do let sources go off the record. But here's where it can bite you. Let's say you're doing an interview with Boynton, and everything is going great … but then he casually holds up a hand and says, "By the way, all that was off the record." All of *what*? How far back in the conversation? How do you qualify that? In an interview, this is usually a red flag. It generally means that the conversation will be peppered with that line. At the end of the day, you'll be left with a pile of confusing notes and the treacherous (and dangerous) job of figuring out what was off the record and what was on it. And after the story prints, your phone will ring and the source will be furious that you published something that was "off the record." Let the record show that this is not the type of source you want to interview.

Rather, once the symptoms begin to develop, try to nip them in the bud. Ask what portion, specifically, was off the record. Gently explain to the source that you want to be sure that you're getting everything off the record and on the record 100 percent right, and, if she's going to tell you something off the record, to please tell you *before* she goes off the record so you can make note of it.

If she doesn't play by the rules, and you're left confused and frustrated, I might cancel the interview and kill the story, or find another source. Sometimes it's just not worth the potential fallout.

THE GHOSTWRITER

I have to admit, this is my most feared source, and the type that has caused me the most hair loss.

This is the source who doesn't know the general rules of nonfiction writing: A piece is the author's piece, and even if it's about the source, it's not owned by the source. The author (and subsequently the editor) has dominion over the article. It's how we are able to write objective pieces for our readers using our knowledge, observation, insight, and expertise.

A few years back, I was working on a piece for a women's magazine about a famous (deceased) artist. I was thrilled to be able to write about him because he was one of my favorite artists. I got in touch with the curator of his archives and explained the concept of the story I wanted to write. The curator wasn't a fan and said he would brainstorm some ideas for the approach and get back to me.

After the call, I had a bad feeling, a growing pit in my gut. My instincts screamed for me to bail. I told my editor that the curator was going to be an epically bad source and that we should consider killing the piece. We eventually agreed to move forward. How bad could he be?

He was flighty and hard to contact, and it took weeks to get an interview with him. Finally, I met him at a smoke-filled warehouse on a prostitute-riddled street, where the artist's archives sat, unkempt. (Warning sign number one, I suppose.) I asked him for digital images of the art for the story, but he couldn't find them on his ancient computer. Every time I would ask an interview question, he would attempt to take the story in a different direction or go on a wild tangent about his RV. Again, the clincher: He had very specific ideas about what he wanted the story to be, and they didn't line up with the simple piece that my editor and I were seeking. He saw the story as his to shape.

I should have left then and never come back.

But I persisted. I wanted to write about the artist. And I needed to see the artist's famous house. It was central to what I was writing. For days or weeks (I can't remember which), the curator deferred. He always had an excuse. Finally, I got him to agree on a day and time, and I drove out. I discovered the artist's house in poor condition, reeking of cat pee. The curator had been living there. I was not allowed to photograph it due to the state of affairs, and I was told photos would be provided instead. I finished the interview (with its fair share of off-the-record moments, of course!) and went home to write it.

It was a simple, short piece, a love letter to the artist.

And then the calls started. The source wanted to see it. I told him that ball was out of my court and that he would have to talk to the editor. He badgered the editor and eventually broke her down. It was sent to him to review his quotes. What could go wrong? I had it all on tape and had written it verbatim using the information he had provided me.

That's when my phone started ringing again. Voice mail after voice mail began pouring in. First, he sounded nervous: "This is a ... this article has very serious issues. Very serious problems. Call me back, Zac."

Each message escalated.

I called him. What was wrong with it? I didn't understand. He didn't like certain wordings. I explained that those were my and the magazine's choices. He claimed I had gotten facts wrong. Which facts? He wasn't sure, but some facts were wrong, he knew. He wanted to change some of his quotes. I explained that I had quoted him verbatim and had tapes of our conversations if he wanted me to play anything back, to show that the facts were exactly as he had stated and that we had independently verified them. He just had a few quotes he'd like to rewrite.

It went on like this for days over tiny aesthetic differences in wording, until I found myself having a panic attack at my home, asking the editor if she would just deal with him and loop me out of the equation.

He had completely broken me down. And it could have all been avoided had I simply trusted my instincts from the start.

All of this is to say: You don't want to work with a source who sees himself as the architect of a piece. Such sources get obsessive and will go to great lengths to gain control of the article. I don't fault them for it: Being an expert on a subject and intimately connected to it, it's hard— and in some cases, impossible—to give up control and trust the writer. Passion can often trump all. But if you sense that your source isn't willing to let you and your editor do your job, you may need to assess the story you're writing and, at minimum, see if you can find a better source who is willing to work with you in a less obsessive capacity.

Otherwise, you may never be able to look at a work by your favorite artist again without seeing the source's grimacing face.

THE SINGLE-ANSWER SOURCE

Phew. Okay. Time to take a step back from that dark saga, take an anxiety pill, apply some Rogain, and discuss an easier source: the single-answer source.

The single-answer source may be providing single answers for a variety of reasons: She may be shy. She may be guarded. She may be paranoid. She may be wary of the media. Regardless, my strategy is always the one outlined earlier: I start off every interview by attempting to put the source at ease and letting her know that I'm just another person—a human!—doing my job, with good motives and good ethics. Then, if the source is still hesitant or guarded in her answers, the best method is to make the interview feel more like a normal conversation rather than an *interview*. Chat. Offer your own thoughts and insights into things. Joke, if the situation warrants it. Be personable, and be human.

When you get a single-word response, ask the follow-ups that will lead to answers that transcend it.

> **ZAC:** What happened that night?
>
> **SOURCE:** The break-in.
>
> **ZAC:** Where were you when it happened?
>
> **SOURCE:** My bedroom.
>
> **ZAC:** How did it make you feel?
>
> **SOURCE:** Scared.
>
> **ZAC:** Understandably. Can you give me an idea of what it was like to be in your room and realize that something like that was happening? A lot of us have never had an experience like that. Can you bring us into the scene to help us fully comprehend what it's really like?
>
> **SOURCE:** I don't like talking about it.
>
> **ZAC:** I fully understand. I can't imagine what it's like to go through something like that. But for readers to really understand what happened, and for us to be able to understand why it led to what it led to, that context really is vital. What was running through your head when you heard the first bang on the door?

THE TANGENTIAL SOURCE

This source is the direct opposite of the single-answer source. When interviewing this type of person, you'll often find a source who is immeasurably passionate, which is a fantastic thing—as long as you can wrangle that enthusiasm and make sense of it for your readers.

ZAC: You've been building this house, brick by brick, alone, for thirty years. It's amazing. When did you decide to start?

SOURCE: It was crazy. It's been my life's work. But I'd be remiss if I didn't at least acknowledge some of the people who have helped me out along the way; it's not like I did everything myself, including mining the materials, forging the brick, and everything like that. John Culver over at Semco Cement was a huge factor in helping to get the supplies; Terry Childers over at Recklinburg Towing was a huge resource in helping me out with a lot of stuff along the way; Jim Levson over at—hang on, I need to make sure I get this right [five-minute pause]—over at Needleman's Building Depot was a huge resource in lumber; and then of course there's the kids. There were so many different kids who I wanted to build this house for, and I know it's taken a long time, but one day they'll be able to call this place home. I just wanted to be able to get the appropriate resources. Ever since I was a kid, I wanted a place like this. Let me tell you, there's a woman over at Shendlen Park who I should tell you about. She and her husband like the house a lot. But still there's this—

ZAC: Can I interrupt for a quick moment? Apologies for butting in. I just want to make sure I understand the origins. Going back to the start, to build a narrative for our readers, when was the first time that the thought of building this house entered your mind—and why?

SOURCE: Of course. I started …

You may never be able to get a simple narrative from an interview, and that's okay. But you *do* want to guide the interview as much as possible and make sure you're getting what you need to be able to reconstruct things and write the piece later. If what you need is sprinkled throughout the article, you'll have to do some digging later, but all the pieces will be there. Passion is by nature reckless, and that's perfectly fine. You just need to be able to make sure you're planting the seeds for a great story and work within its often chaotic confines.

THE HATER

We touched on this one a bit earlier. Here's how I would handle such an interaction.

> **ZAC:** Thanks again for taking the time to talk. Can you tell me a bit about your new project in 2016?
>
> **SOURCE:** I'll be real with you: I don't like the media. I've been misquoted time and again. Your paper has taken several idiotic stances in the last year. I hate writers, and I don't want to do this, because I know how it'll end up.
>
> **ZAC:** I'm sorry you've had those experiences, and I surely regret you have those feelings toward *The Daily Eagle*. But please know that I'm just here to write about the project lineup that you have on deck for next year. I can't speak to any of the stances that the paper has taken, but I can assure you that I'm a good journalist and that the last thing I'll do is misquote you, be unfair, or write a story that isn't completely sound.
>
> **SOURCE:** You don't sound all that bad.
>
> **ZAC:** Give me a chance to change your idea of writers.

Or:

> **ZAC:** Thanks for taking the time to take my call. I really appreciate it.
>
> **SOURCE:** I just answered so I could tell you how much I hate the liberal media[9] and your magazine. Screw you. You'll get no interview from me.
>
> **ZAC:** Was that on the record?
>
> **SOURCE:** You bet your ass.
>
> **ZAC:** Okay. Thanks for your time. Give me a call back if you change your mind or would like to talk.[10]

Pick your battles carefully—and know which ones are predetermined.

---

9 For what it's worth, let the record show that I have had about a fifty-fifty conservative/liberal boss ratio over the years.

10 You're awful.

THE DISAPPEARING ACT

This type of source is actually more common than one might think.

The most frequent (and damaging!) instance of this, for me, has always been a source who does an interview but is unreachable when you have a key follow-up question later. He doesn't answer the phone. He doesn't reply to e-mails. He seems to have disappeared from the face of the earth.

In these situations, I start out with an e-mail, and then, depending on the deadline, I follow up soon after with a phone call.

The text is simple enough:

> Dear James,
> Thanks so much for taking the time to do the interview last week. I've been attempting to get in touch with you about some important last-minute details needed for the piece, but I haven't been able to reach you by phone or e-mail.
>
> I know your schedule is incredibly busy at the moment, but it's extremely important to the piece and would only take about five minutes to cover on the phone. My deadline is coming up Friday, so I would love to touch base as soon as you have a moment.
>
> Many thanks in advance for your time, James, and hope all is well.
>
> Zac

LIES AND THE LYING LIARS WHO TELL THEM

Often, when fact-checking interviews, you might discover that a source had a date off by a couple of years, got the name of the restaurant wrong, etc. Stuff like that is normal.

But what do you do when you know a source is lying to your face or misleading you?

Let's say you're writing about a dispute between two restaurant owners. You've done your research and know the story pretty well: Two brothers went into business together but had a crazy falling-out because one owner slept with the other's wife. They since opened two competing restaurants and have been conducting infantile acts of vandalism against each other, escalating with each retaliation.

One brother, Ken, told you on the record that his sibling, Paul, paid a cook to put crickets in Ken's deep fryer. They were subsequently served to customers, prompting the health department and police to get involved. Ken told you this. But then the cook also revealed this on the record, and you have the police report and have spoken to the health department and verified the situation.

So now you're interviewing Paul:

> **ZAC:** I'd like to talk about the cricket incident.
>
> **PAUL:** That's all baloney.
>
> **ZAC:** Do you mean it didn't happen, or that the situation has been blown out of proportion, or something along those lines?
>
> **PAUL:** Ken's a liar. He put the crickets in there himself and then paid the cook.

At this point, Paul doesn't know you have official reports on the incident. He also doesn't know that the cook has made a sworn affidavit, taken a polygraph, and admitted his wrongdoing in accepting cash for crickets.

> **ZAC:** Paul, are you denying that you had any involvement in that?
>
> **PAUL:** Yes.
>
> **ZAC:** From what I've read and researched—
>
> **PAUL:** Are you calling me a liar?
>
> **ZAC:** No, I didn't say that. I was going to say that I have official documents in which the cook claimed that you paid him money to put the crickets in the fryer.
>
> **PAUL:** [Silence.]
>
> **ZAC:** I'm just looking for your side of the story. Word of that will be coming out soon, from what I have been told, and if you would like to discuss the situation, I'd like to talk to you about it.
>
> **PAUL:** [Pause.] Well, last week …

Of course, a conversation like this is not always so cut-and-dried. If you suspect someone is misleading you, dig into the situation and investigate. Always quote the person who is telling you his side of the story, versus putting it in the article as fact coming from you, the author. Dig until you have the truth and it has been corroborated, and don't write a word until you do.

A NOTE ON THE VULNERABLE SOURCE

First, let me be clear: The vulnerable source is *not* a problem source. But it is a source that merits discussion. One of my first assignments as a newbie reporter was to interview the widow of a man who had died of West Nile Virus. Later, I was tasked with interviewing the relatives of a young marine killed in action. Later, I spoke with a marine badly disfigured by an IED. Later, it was the parents of a dying child.

Nothing prepares you for these types of interviews. Moreover, there's no playbook for them.

My best advice: Be human. Be gentle. Respect boundaries. If a source wants to share her story with you, listen. If she doesn't, never force her to.

Sometimes you have to be a person before a writer.

Let your inner compass guide you.

CHAPTER 7

WALKING THE WALK

"The road to hell is paved with works-in-progress."

—PHILIP ROTH

"The road to hell is paved with adverbs."

—STEPHEN KING

"It ain't whatcha write, it's the way atcha write it."

—JACK KEROUAC

Now, at long last, we get to the marrow of what you came here to do in the first place: Write!

While I don't have the page count to go into an überdetailed how-to for every single type of article, we're going to cover the most prevalent, the best practices of which can carry over into many other types of pieces. What follows are tips and tricks, some notes on structure, and examples of the articles in form.

But before we begin, let's cover a few basics of the writing game.

TENSE: Generally newspaper articles will be written in past tense, and articles for magazine and magazine-style outlets will be written in present tense.[1] Think *said* versus *says*. Why the dichotomy? I've always regarded newspaper pieces as a record of the times—marked with a definitive past-tense annotation of authority. Magazines, however, publish far less often, so you might see it as our desperate attempt to remain relevant, even though the stories you're reading were actually written months ago. Smoke screen!

STYLE: As I mentioned, publications tend to use their own house styles first and then, most commonly, AP Style, the industry standard. My best advice is to study *The Associated Press Stylebook* and then begin incorporating it naturally into your work as you edit what you've written. Adhering to a journalistic standard is a good practice for any freelancer.

You can get the *Stylebook* in a variety of forms: in a spiral-bound print edition (ever-useful for on-the-go editing), in an online subscription edition (worth the price alone for the ability to quickly search different words, preventing you from having to thumb through the book hundreds of thousands of times in your career), and in a smartphone app.

Here are some of the core rules of AP Style. It's not a bad idea to start internalizing them now.

- For numerical references, generally spell out *one* through *nine*, and start using figures at *10*.
- That being said, age is always a number in AP Style: "a 1-year-old."

---

1 But, of course, to make things even more confusing, newspaper headlines will be written in the present tense. Welcome to the bizarre world of publishing!

- AP has a whole list of alternate state abbreviations to ruin everything you know about two-letter state references. Use these in the body copy of your article. (*Tenn.* vs. *TN*, *Mass.* vs. *MA*, *Maine* vs. *ME*.)
- To further complicate matters, some cities must be accompanied by their states when referenced, and others—bigger, more recognizable cities—stand alone. Think *Los Angeles*, *Denver*, *Chicago*, or even *Cincinnati*, but *Tiffin, Ohio*.
- The *Stylebook* is quite particular about the use of quotation marks. In AP, you put quotation marks around song titles, book titles, etc., but not magazine titles or newspaper titles.
- Use a person's first and last name upon "first reference" (the first time he or she appears in the story), and then simply use the last name for all subsequent references.
- Ditch the "Mr." and "Ms." This isn't *The New York Times*. Unless, of course, it is *The New York Times*, in which case the house style is to keep the awkward courtesy titles.
- Use only one space after a sentence. Let that publication jam as much text into their limited print space as possible. (And start writing this way. An editor will quickly question your game if you deliver a piece with two spaces between sentences. Though, it's worth noting, very famous authors have written pieces for me with double-spacing between sentences. So this is more of a nitpicky editor preference than anything.)
- If a person's title comes before her name in your story, capitalize the title: "Print magazine Editor-in-Chief Zachary Petit." But lowercase the title if it comes after the name: "'I was just whining about double-spacing after sentences,' says Zachary Petit, editor in chief of Print magazine."
- Celebrate the fact that AP has come into the twenty-first century. The last few years have brought promising strides: *E-mail* is now formatted as *email*, and *Web site* is now just *website*. Hooray!

The *AP Stylebook* inventories rules galore. But they're worth following. Editors value (and are rightly obsessed with) *consistency*. If every reference in a magazine were formatted differently, we'd look like we were doing one hell of a bad job at editing. Resources like the *AP Stylebook* (and our own house styles) ensure that we adhere to standards of quality and present our body of work as a cohesive whole.[2]

VERSATILITY AND FLEXIBILITY: Don't limit yourself to just one form. I've known writers who specialize in a single form (the Q&A, the profile) and refuse (or don't know how) to write in another form. While some have made a name for themselves doing so, it's a bad idea. Sure, you can *specialize* in a form, but don't be so stubborn as to let it completely define your work. The writer who is talented can excel and learn all forms—which makes you a hell of a lot more useful a freelancer than a scribe versed in one form. Let's say I need a good feature story about a new bar that's opening and the talented, world-renowned bartenders who work there. My best writer—the magazine's flagship writer—is available, but I don't want it in Q&A format, which she exclusively writes. So I'd call up Writer B, who may not be as good as Writer A, but is open to writing anything.

Write everything under the sun. Write long. Write short. Write in first person, third person, and, hey, if you're feeling especially adventurous, second person.

Become versatile. And become a pro at everything within your versatile stable.

Then, no matter what an editor approaches you with, you'll be able to play ball.

And moreover, you'll grow. The more challenges you take on, the better you'll become.

THE SHORT GAME: FRONT OF THE BOOK

Truth be told, writing short—and truly short—is some of the hardest writing you can do. I have a tendency to write long, which may be part of my reasoning here, but I truly believe it. To distill a subject to its very essence, and to do so with clarity, style, and, often, humor, is no easy feat. It takes every ounce of a writer's talent. When I've praised editors

---

2 The astute, nerdy fellow reader will notice that this book does not follow AP Style. That's because WD Books (and a slew of other book publishers) use the *Chicago Manual of Style*. Maybe one day all of us editors will unite in Geneva and agree to a peace treaty on a singular style. Until that day, the fight continues …

on my team for their front-of-the-book pieces and said that not many people can do what they do, I've meant every word of it.

BASIC STRUCTURE

Of course, structure depends heavily on what you're writing. Let's start with a basic filler piece, like this one I wrote for *Writer's Digest* a few years back. Again, as in the examples referenced earlier, I include my own work here not as a shining pinnacle of perfection in form but rather because I know exactly what went into these pieces and how they were crafted.

IN MEMORIAM

Cormac McCarthy's Typewriter, 1963-2009

In the early '60s, a young writer stopped by a Tennessee pawnshop and paid $50 for an Olivetti manual typewriter. It was reliable, to say the least: Over the next nearly five decades, Cormac McCarthy banged out an estimated 5 million words on it. All of his books—think *Blood Meridian*, *No Country for Old Men*, *All the Pretty Horses*, *The Road*, etc.—and even three unpublished works spawned from the secondhand purchase. As rare book dealer Glenn Horowitz told *The New York Times*, "It's as if Mount Rushmore was carved with a Swiss Army knife."

Late last year, after it began to show "serious signs of wear," McCarthy put the typewriter up for auction, with the proceeds benefiting the Sante Fe Institute (an organization focused on research to bolster scientific understanding).

The typewriter was expected to fetch between $15,000 and $20,000, but when the auction drew to a close, it brought in a hulking $254,000.

McCarthy's replacement: appropriately, another Olivetti.

And why not? With a 46-year clean bill of health—"It has never been serviced or cleaned other than blowing out the dust with a service station airhose," the author wrote in his certificate of authenticity—5 million words and a 507,900 percent markup, they really just don't make 'em like that any more.

BREAKDOWN

Regardless of the length of your story, what you want to do is *tell* a story. Some stories require 20,000 words. Others, such as the one above, require only about 200. When writing in such small space, make sure you begin with a catching lead. Without it, there's a good chance your reader may not get past the first twenty words. Here I attempted to build intrigue by introducing McCarthy not as the legend he is today but as a young writer picking up a typewriter in the machine's heyday at a pawnshop. The fact that the bolded lead-in text (1963-2009) included a wide date range lends it intrigue.

Next, I delved deeper into the meat of the intrigue: All of his books were written on the same cheap machine, with a quote from a reputable source bringing the magnitude of that fact into focus.

Finally, I get to the point of the piece—what makes it "newsworthy" and gives it a hook: The typewriter was sold at auction, and for an eye-opening amount. At the end, I introduce elements of humor (the service station air hose) and have the simple kick that McCarthy replaced it with the same (now-antiquated) device. Throughout the piece, precise details—specific amounts and a host of proper nouns—give weight and legitimacy to a short article, allowing it to have more impact and get its point across.

A quick read and a simple (and equally quick) write.

TIPS

When writing front-of-the-book content keep the following in mind:

WRITE TIGHT. But don't obsess over it. Know your word count, and then write as you normally would. For me, that means jotting down 600 words for a 250-word piece and then mercilessly cutting.

Speaking of cutting: How do you know what to keep? I always paste the assignment notes from my editor into my working doc. Even if it's just a sentence about what she wants written and the tone she wants it written in, I use it as a guiding light to help me grit my teeth and kill my darlings so I can deliver on the most basic bare bones of the assignment.

DON'T THINK YOU CAN ABANDON STRUCTURE JUST BE-CAUSE YOU'RE WORKING ON A SHORT PIECE. Structure is especially ornate in tiny pieces. Consider a large dinner table. It might consist of only six solid pieces of wood that make up the whole. Now consider a watch and all the intricate doodads inside.

Circular structures—mentioning something at the start and then circling back to it at the end—can be highly effective in short pieces. It gives them the feeling of a concise, well-assembled whole. (And the callback is even more effective since it's usually only spaced out between a couple of paragraphs or so.)

I used to write a column for *Writer's Digest* called "Top Shelf," which featured a handful of neat products around the writing world. Here's an entry in the "Bookshelf Edition" installment I penned. Again, this isn't high literature but a functional example of how callbacks can bring the whole thing together. (The bolded terms in this excerpt demonstrate its circular structure.)

> If space is at a premium in your home (e.g., you're trying to make it in publishing in **New York**), and you want something a bit out of the box, check out ThinkGeek's Hidden Bookshelf—a bookshelf without a bookshelf. Thanks to a simple metal wedge, 20 pounds worth of books look like they're floating in a stack on your wall. Which saves space ... and looks darn cool in the process. Not included: $1,400/month **Manhattan** studio apartment.

DON'T BE AFRAID TO SHOWCASE VOICE IN YOUR PIECE, SHOULD IT FIT WITH THE MAGAZINE'S EDITORIAL STYLE. As with the previous example, which sought to emulate the "savvy/laid-back/insider/writerly" voice throughout the column, it can be an effective way to match that magazine's feel and have some fun in the process.

Likewise, don't be afraid to inject some humor into your piece, should it fit with the magazine's editorial voice.

PLAYING IT STRAIGHT: THE BASIC NEWSPAPER STORY

Writing a news story is an exercise in discipline. The emphasis is on the facts—getting to them as fast as possible, informing your readers, throwing in a few quotes to liven things up, and then getting the hell out as fast as possible.

I'll admit: The rigidity of the form has always been a turnoff for me, and working as a news reporter is one of the hardest things I have done. But the exercise in discipline is fantastic, one that imbues you with an array of strong writing mechanics you can use later. It's one of those "you must know the rules before you can break them" scenarios.

Moreover, a creative writer can play well within the form and bend the accepted rules to her advantage. At the end of the day, if the story gets a reader's attention and properly informs, you've done your job. It's up to your editor how much he'll let you frolic in the field of his pages.

BASIC STRUCTURE

News stories are written in what's called the Inverted Pyramid Structure. Picture an upside-down pyramid, with the bulkiest part at the top. The best visual breakdown I've seen simply divided the pyramid into three parts: The top is "most important," the middle is "less important," and the very bottom (the tip) is "least important."

The basic idea is to give readers the key information first, so that, should they stop reading early on in the article, they will have already gleaned the point. The strategic element of an inverted pyramid is that it allows an editor to simply cut from the bottom up, should he need to do so for space.

As for the structure itself, news stories follow this pattern, in this order:

Lede

The lede (pronounced "leed") is, essentially, your first sentence—the one that must hook readers and inform them in a compelling way what the story will be about. Your mission here is to educate and to do so in a way that gets the red medicine of reading a bland news story down smoothly. Educators commonly advise a maximum length of around thirty words, and the briefer or punchier you can make it, the better. A 2000 Scripps study of a wide sampling of U.S. newspapers found the average lede to be 23.5 words.

A lede should be penned in active voice. It should read easily. It should capture attention. And to be effective, it should not be bogged down by a half-dozen proper nouns, as in the following example.

> Investigators of the National Society of Oceanic Standards, citing a study by the National Ocean Cognitive Collective, said Saturday that one in every five species of endangered Blue Shell Tortoises on the Oswego Island off Madagascar come into contact with Shell Oil on a daily basis, thanks to a new rig capacity problem on the Shell Discovery Mark V.

Instead, why not:

> Life for the endangered Blue Shell Tortoise just got a lot harder.

The possibilities for your lede depend on how quickly you can cover the basic facts in your ...

Nutgraph

Since journalists obsessed with consistency ironically can't agree on the spelling of basic terminology in their own field (*lead* vs. *lede*, for instance), it should be said that you'll see the nutgraph referred to as *nutgraf*, *nut graf*, *nut graph*, and so on. But it all means the same thing: a paragraph that covers the essentials of the story—everything a reader needs to know—and serves as the "in a nutshell" version of the article. It follows the lede.

For the story in the previous example, you could get away with a simpler lede by making sure the nutgraph is up to snuff:

> Life for the endangered Blue Shell Tortoise just got a lot harder.
> Investigators at the National Society of Oceanic Standards have released a new study showing that the already beleaguered reptilian faces a new threat as a result of a leaking oil rig off the shores of Madagascar. The study states that one in five tortoises, native to the Oswego Islands, will come into contact with raw oil from the Shell Discovery Mark V on a daily basis.

Quote

After your nutgraph, it's common practice to deploy your first quote. Obviously, it should be compelling and should back up or complement the hook in your lede and nutgraph while, ideally, adding something new to further the story and serve as a transition to the rest of the piece. Finding the right quote for your story is like putting on a tailored glove: It must be a perfect fit.

> "They're called Blue Shell Tortoises, right?" said NSOS field researcher Tom Owens. "Problem is, soon enough you're not going to see blue ones—you're going to see black ones. And that's just the beginning."

Everything Else

From there, your story will be filled out with secondary details, more quotes, and so on. Regardless of what constitutes this "everything else," make sure you cover, as early as possible (especially in a nutgraph and lede), the five *W*s—who, what, where, when, and why. These make up the core of news articles, though the last one—the "why"—may be the unknown in your piece and can be the hardest to pin down.

Kick

I'm of the mind-set that a strong kick—the last sentence of the piece—can be as important to overall form and impact as a lede. Good kicks are artful. They offer a perfect final thought on the previous 500 words, and can include humor, irony, or even a bit of perspective from the writer.

They commonly take two forms: a quote, or a closing thought or bit of info from the writer. As for finding a good kick: Review your notes. What last word sums it all up perfectly? What fact offers a final parting insight on the topic? You'll know the kick when you see it. I often identify a kick the moment I read through my interview transcripts, and I mark it for later so I know what I'm working toward in the piece. A good kick cannot be undervalued or thrown in on a whim. It's the invaluable Last Word, and it's the veritable wax seal on your piece.

Here's an example of a quote kick that employs a callback.

> "Well, Shell can say whatever they want to say," he said. "But all I know is, unless they change the color of their oil, the Blue Shell Tortoise is going to remain black."

Now, employing this structural model, let's do what you should never do in the news business and make up a story.

> TOLEDO, OHIO — A beloved Randolph Theater ticket-taker is missing his first show in five decades tonight, and for good reason: He's in jail.
>
> On Monday, Toledo police arrested Oscar Boynton, 63, of Harvard Terrace, citing criminal activity loosely related to the ongoing "Chirpgate" feud between restaurateurs Ken Karver and Paul Karver. Boynton was taken into custody at the Randolph Theater prior to the evening performance of "Grease!"
>
> "Today Oscar Boynton didn't take any tickets," Officer Barry Williams said. "Instead, I punched his."
>
> As of press time, the specific details of the arrest are unclear. By 8 P.M. Monday, numerous theater patrons and the cast of "Grease!" had assembled outside the county jail with "FREE BOYNTON" signs to demand the specifics of his detention.
>
> The Toledo Police Department has refused to comment, other than confirming that the arrest is indeed related to the Karver brothers' feud.
>
> "Yes, this is Chirpgate, and the alleged crimes are very serious," Chief Randy Jonsel said. "All we can say at this time is that there are some very salacious things that will likely come out over the next few weeks."
>
> On Jan. 12, 2014, brothers Ken Karver and Paul Karver announced they were ending their longstanding partnership of the popular downtown restaurant Cluckers. A public falling out ensued, with Ken retaining ownership of the restaurant. Six months later, Paul opened his own competing restaurant across the street on Vine Parkway, and the two began committing a series of mischievous acts against each other. Said acts climaxed when police arrested Paul for putting crickets in Ken's deep fryer, drawing the attention of the Toledo Health Department.
>
> While Boynton's exact involvement remains unknown, protesters Monday demanded answers.
>
> "What did Oscar do?" asked Geoffrey Lord, an accountant from Harvard Terrace. "He takes tickets. He doesn't distribute crickets. This must end."
>
> Others on the scene were less supportive, such as Seth Neeley, one of the many patrons who consumed the fried crickets at Cluckers earlier this year.

"I tell you, if he was part of the crew who fed me crickets, you sure as hell better believe that I'll be buying a ticket to 'Grease!' and giving him a piece of my mind," Neeley said. "He'll be eating crickets before all this is over."

DYEING YOUR DACHSHUND: THE HOW-TO

As anyone with an Internet connection and a problem knows, there's a *lot* of bad advice out there.

Think back to the last time you wanted to know how to fix your kitchen sink. Or replace your toilet tank. Or do something more outside the ordinary, like, say, safely dye your dog's fur green so he could be Yoda for Halloween.

You typed your quandary into Google in search of a solid how-to— and up popped ten thousand unreliable websites that specialize in how-tos but offer less-than-stellar advice. This deluge of (poorly written!) and often downright inaccurate info makes a lot of us journalists see red (not to mention whatever poor dachshund is about to be turned green). But there's one good thing to come of all this: *It means great how-tos are more valuable than ever.*

How-tos, or *service pieces*, as they're often called, are simple and fast to write, and everyone from newspapers to magazines to websites publishes them—which makes them an excellent gateway to breaking into a publication.

So let's do our civic duties as journalists and save the kitchen sinks and dachshunds of the world.

Rather than follow our usual format established above, Here is a how-to on how to write a how-to.

1. CHOOSE YOUR ADVENTURE.

First, you have to pick a compelling topic. So brainstorm away. This is actually one of the easiest parts of the process: Just start with your expertise. Again, consider: What do you know in a way that nobody else does? Flex that knowledge. Then brainstorm more and consider what problems you've recently solved. Tap into your own curiosity, and chances are you'll tap into someone else's. Or, again, choose a big story—say, a swine flu outbreak story you saw on CNN—and turn it into a small piece: how to tell if you've got swine flu, regular flu, bird flu, a cold, or hypochondria.

2. DO YOUR HOMEWORK.

What's it going to take to pull this piece off successfully? Make a list. Then bang out a rough draft.

Ask yourself: Do you have enough knowledge to write it on your own? Even if you think you do, go deeper: What links and resources can you provide to readers who are looking for supplemental info? Would the piece be enriched by quotes from experts or statistics you've dug up? Even if you know exactly what you're talking about, people like to see a chorus of consensus.

3. KNOW YOUR READER.

Determine whom your piece is intended for: the expert, the layperson, the dabbler, the desperate Googler, or all of them at once. Craft your material to that specific person or group—and remember, if you're writing for a daily newspaper, it will indeed be for all readers at once—and consider *showing* your rough draft to someone who fits that description. Does it all make sense to him and get him where he needs to go?

4. BE DEEP.

There's nothing worse for a reader than finding a how-to on exactly the topic you're seeking, and then realizing that it consists of bare bones, overly obvious basics totaling 75 words. So anticipate all the questions your reader may have, and answer them now. Be like narrative nonfiction author Richard Ben Cramer, who said, "I'm out there to clean the plate. Once they've read what I've written on a subject, I want them to think, 'That's it!' I think the highest aspiration people in our trade can have is that once they've written a story, nobody will ever try it again." Sure, writing Pulitzer-grade prose on conflicts in the Middle East is slightly different than writing a 500-word story on how to keep squirrels off your birdfeeder, but the same principle applies to all good work.

5. BE DEEP ... BUT BE CAREFUL.

Like a diver, the deeper you go, the more pressure is on you. You have to get everything in your how-to correct. Don't trust the Internet. Your own experience with your subject, as well as the input of experts, is much more reliable. Fact-check everything; field-test everything. Getting it right builds trust with editors and, moreover, with readers, who will be embarking upon the very experiment you're proposing.

6. BE CHRONOLOGICAL.

This step probably should have come a few paragraphs ago in this how-to. But still. It'll make your piece exponentially easier for readers to follow.

7. BE SUCCINCT.

Yup.

8. POLISH TO PERFECTION.

As in all writing, this is vital, but especially here. If you're writing a piece about how to view the meteor shower happening next weekend, and you make an obvious gaffe like misspelling *meteor* or getting the name of a constellation wrong, not many people are going to trust your suggestions for the best viewing locations around town.

9. SEAL THE DEAL.

Finally, make sure you *finish* the piece and actually submit it. Cast your fears aside, and put your work in someone's hands, trusting she might want to know *exactly* what you've just written.

You should overanalyze your piece, but not so much that it never leaves your desktop. After all, as Philip Roth said, "The road to hell is paved with works-in-progress."

And hell is a long way away from that meteor shower everyone wants to see.

QUIZ SHOW: THE Q&A

I love Q&As. I used to dislike doing them because I felt they were boring for writers. You ask a set of questions; you run the responses. Done. But it's not that simple, and once you get into them, you realize how much of an art form they really are. They engage your inner editor, and soon enough, you realize it takes a lot of work to compile a good one. They're more of an editing challenge than a writing one, and, done well, they can be some of the best pieces out there.

BASIC STRUCTURE

While pulling off an excellent Q&A is complicated work, the structure is the easy part. Generally, Q&As involve an introduction that establishes the subject and his background and contains the hook of the conversation. (What's newsworthy about this subject? Why would a reader want to listen to him ramble for the next few pages? Why, in a nutshell, are you writing about him?) The questions and answers follow the intro, and then you're done. These pieces sometimes involve sidebars, but that depends on the info you obtain from the subject, the needs of the publication, and so on.

The following is a Q&A I did last year for *Print* magazine. The subject was Neal Adams, a legendary comic book artist and creator known for his big personality and outspokenness. Adams was going to be at a comic convention in Louisville, Kentucky, so I got a press pass, drove down to the event, found Adams at his booth, and asked him for an interview later in the day, or later yet by phone.

"Have a seat," he said. "Let's do it now."

Adams's giant table was bustling with fans buying art and asking him to sign it—not exactly the controlled environment of question and answer that makes for a good piece. I was hesitant, but I sat down next to him, turned on my recorder, and proceeded to ask him questions about his life, career, and work. Problem was, Adams is prone to rambling (and I mean that in a good way—he's fascinating to talk to), and for every question I asked, two or three fans would come up to get something signed. It went on like this for two hours, until I called it a day and went in search of some *Doctor Who* trinkets, thinking the whole article would be an unusable mess. He had given me some great quotes and insights, but would the sum of the parts actually read as a conversation, bearing in mind the interview had been interrupted close to one hundred times?

I considered trashing it. But then I transcribed it and Frankensteined it together.

Did I pull it off? You be the judge.

STUBBORN. AGGRESSIVE. POSITIVE.

Legendary artist and writer Neal Adams talks creators' rights, social issues in art and—of course—comics, sans filter.

Originally published in Print, *October 2014*

The thing about Neal Adams is he doesn't really come across as the most, well, modest man.

"Your work is pretty amazing," a young fan gushes to Adams at a recent comic convention.

"I've noticed that," Adams replies. "I have noticed that."

The 73-year-old comic book writer and artist is opinionated, outspoken, wildly talented, engaging, a born cusser and a born hustler (you should see him hawking his artwork at these conventions). And that's all undoubtedly how he's been in the game so long.

Adams soldiered past initial barriers to the industry and became a legendary talent for both Marvel and DC, leaving his stylistic mark on such iconic series as Batman, the X-Men, Green Lantern and Superman. He co-founded the design studio Continuity Associates. Along the way, he became known as much for his work as his activism: For decades, he's battled for the rights of creators, winning Jerry Siegel and Joe Shuster—who sold their character Superman to DC for a paltry $130 in the 1930s—long overdue compensation and credit.

For his life's work, he's received numerous awards, and has been inducted into the Will Eisner Hall of Fame (the industry's highest honor) alongside legends Jack Kirby and Stan Lee.

No, Neal Adams is probably not best described as modest. But he's one of those rare people who might just have a right not to be.

You had an incredibly difficult time breaking in. How did you persevere?

I got better jobs. I worked for a place called Johnstone and Cushing, and we did comics for advertising and I was paid four to six times as much as a regular comic book artist. I did storyboards for advertising agencies, and I got paid better than any comic book artist got paid. I did illustration work, and I got paid better. It was a source of embarrassment that somebody would ask me what I was going to charge them and then they became quiet for a minute and said, "Well, I don't think our accounting department will pay a bill that's that low. We have to pay you more."

Did it ever get you down, how difficult it was to get your portfolio read?

If I get rejected, I just come back. Look, there's nobody within the comic business that's five years my junior or five years my senior. There's nobody in comics that's a contemporary of mine. They don't exist. There's 10 years of *blank*. So obviously I was a very stubborn, aggressive, positive person. You don't get to be somebody like me without being very, very tough.

Looking at the industry today, what are new artists' chances of breaking in?

Are you kidding? This is like f***ing gold times. It's the easiest time in the world to break in—if you're incredibly talented. The thing you have to remember is there's an art student or an art guy in every junior high school and high school across the country. And there are tens of thousands of them. There aren't that many jobs. ... It's a very, very tough field. And it's getting tougher because the illustration field is going away. There's very little real illustration being done in America today. Movie posters are photographs. Where is *The Saturday Evening Post* or *Life* magazine? They're gone. Illustrators now are doing comics. The very best artists in America and in the world are doing comic books.

From among all the characters you've worked on over the years, which rank as your favorites, creatively?

I like Batman because I was able to bring him to what he was supposed to be. I didn't change him. I just brought him back to what he was supposed to be—[away from the campy nostalgia of the TV show, and back to brooding]. I created Havok out of whole cloth, so that's pretty interesting. I took Green Arrow, who was a copy of Batman, and turned him into his own independent-type character that you never saw before. So in effect I created Green Arrow, yet I'm stuck with the fact that I re-created Green Arrow. For Green Lantern, I didn't do anything except make him the character that Gil Kane created and saved him from obscurity, and then created John Stewart [in the early '70s], who is a black Green Lantern, and I gave a character for black American kids and kids around the world to look up to.

You approach race and social issues a fair amount in your work, and don't pull punches. What's comics' role?
I think the role of comic books is to be the adults while we're being children. We have to look to our children, at our children growing up and what kind of world they're going to be in, and try to reproduce that world in the art that we do so that the world will get there. If we don't show some of that world, then our kids will never get there. We're so close to the ground level with comic books that we're actually having an effect. I've had black men cry in front of me because of John Stewart. Just the impact. Other people may not think that much of it, but he appears on television to millions and millions of people.

What's it like to see your ideas so deeply saturated into popular culture?
It's like being a movie star without being recognized on the street. It's pretty good. When I come [to conventions], they treat me like I'm something and they get all flustered and sweaty, and that's what they do with the actors. But when I go out on the street, nobody knows who I am. So I have the best of all possible worlds, because who the hell wants that?

Do you think people in general tend to overlook the value, impact and influence of creators?
No. I think that what happens is nobody realizes what's gonna happen right at the beginning. At the beginning it's just, "Yeah, yeah, fine, I'll pay you for it." Later on when it takes off suddenly, corporations and people start to get protective, and then aggressively protective, and suddenly they want the whole pie and they don't want to share it because the pie's getting bigger and bigger and bigger. Superman was like that. Nobody knew Superman would become fantastic. Between the ages of 17 and 21, [Siegel and Shuster] failed

to sell it to anybody and they were just busy working, and finally DC Comics agreed to run it, and then newsstands went nuts. And within a year, they were selling a million copies. Well, that's like unheard of. So now that quick little agreement that was given to Jerry Siegel and Joe Shuster became life and death for DC Comics, and became a problem for the rest of the lives of Jerry and Joe.

What's one thing you wish you'd known going into all this?
If something happens, sometimes I back off and I stay back, and I think about it and then I react to it. I've made so many mistakes, there's not one that I can point to. Tons and tons of mistakes and stupid things and ridiculous things, but usually I make stories of them. When I do something really stupid, I say to my family, "OK, remember this whenever anybody says your father's a genius. Because your father's a f***ing idiot. Remember that."

TIPS

When writing and editing Q&As:

TAKE FULL ADVANTAGE OF YOUR INTRO. This is the only place in your Q&A where you'll be able to have your say, offer your insight into the subject, and flex your writing muscles. Cover the basics, of course: who your subject is, why you're writing about her, and so on. But then try to take things a bit deeper and on a broader scale.

Since you have the floor before you hand the mic to your interview subject, what can you tell readers that they might not pick up in the Q&A—or something that perhaps they should know going into it? Think insight. Think personality traits.

In this case, I was struck by how blunt, opinionated, and sometimes even off-putting Neal Adams was in our conversation. It came across that way in the original, unedited text, too, so I decided to directly acknowledge it and use it as a framing device. (The first line, before I took it back a notch, was "Neal Adams is an asshole." The kick would have been the same concept as it printed—"But he's one of those rare people who just might have a right to be one.")

If you poke around the Internet, you'll quickly find innumerable people calling Neal Adams out for being much the same. To overlook that fact felt like an omission. And, as fate would have it, he began our conversation acting the part—but then reversed course and lapsed into self-deprecation at the end, which gave deeper context on his character, transcended the often one-dimensional perspective of his personality, and brought things, in their own way, full circle.

DO MULTIPLE PASSES OF YOUR Q&A. You'll have to read it numerous times to get a good feel for what works and what doesn't—and how you can shape the clay into a nice piece. If possible, I'll take a week off after the interview to gain some distance—and thus objectivity. Then I'll transcribe it and do a few initial reads of the raw transcript to get a sense of the flow, where things get tangential, and so on. After that, I'll save a new version of the file. In this case, NealAdams1.doc was followed by NealAdams2.doc, and so on. You never want to save over your full transcript, because you'll need to reference it later to fact-check, make sure you have it in the right order, make sure you haven't taken anything out of context, and so on. On the next passes I'll highlight in yellow the parts that are "musts": the questions and responses I need to include, either because they adhere to what the editor was seeking in the original assignment or simply because this material is strongest. Then I'll highlight in green the "maybes," should I have the space, and highlight in red the parts that can or should be cut. From there, I'll edit accordingly to bring down the piece to the correct word count.

EDIT CAREFULLY, AND HONESTLY. This is where punctuation marks like ellipses and brackets come into play. When editing a Q&A, you're faced with a tricky task: Make it readable for your audience, make it flow well, but keep it in context and true to what the source said and how he intended to say it.

Let's say you have this sentence:

> He said, well, he meant to say, I think—I think he meant to say, "What you did was wrong."

True human speech, recorded exactly, can be a cluttered mess. With this sentence you might want to keep the full thing, as stated, to reflect the sense of disorder and chaos in the subject's mind regarding whatever situation he is describing. But if it's not important to the context of the question you asked, and he was merely tripping over his own speech, you could chop the first part and run it as:

> I think he meant to say, "What you did was wrong."

Let's say you're low on space, and you have this sentence:

> Rachel was going down to the kitchen to make some cookies. Cookies are pretty good. We always used to eat them. Every Christmas we'd eat them, and they were always nice. She came back up later with the cookies and ...

Here's where an ellipses could come into play. In interviews, ellipses indicate to the reader that something has been cut. Some editors I know will cut portions of text and not include them, but I tend to keep them to maintain honesty with the reader, and so the source feels comfortable that I let readers know that I truncated some of his words.

For instance:

> Rachel was going down to the kitchen to make some cookies. ... She came back up later with the cookies and ...

Some editors I know will also edit quotes for house style. I don't do this, as I believe it takes away from the manner in which things were actually phrased in an interview, which is a very human, and telling, detail. Until recently, AP Style was to use "more than" instead of "over" to express "greater than." So an editor might format:

> "He ate over 200 cookies!" Smith said.

As:

> "He ate more than 200 cookies!" Smith said.

Would anyone actually misread that as he was literally eating something else while floating above two hundred cookies? For the most part I keep phrases intact, as the interview subject stated them, unless they're confusing. In those cases, I clarify the text with brackets. Brackets are used by writers to indicate that they replaced a word the subject originally said with a word of her own, often for clarity.

For example, I would change this sentence:

> John took his dog to the vet. Carl was sick.

To:

> John took his dog to the vet. [His Chihuahua], Carl, was sick.

Or:

> John took his dog, [Carl], to the vet. Carl was sick.

Bracketed text can also be used to replace incorrect words or references stated by a subject so you can avoid presenting inaccurate info to readers. Your source will often thank you for not simply using "(SIC)"—Latin for *sic erat scriptum*, "thus was it written"—to shame them for improper use of a word.

I also use bracketed tags, when appropriate, to give the reader a sense of the interviewee's personality or to convey how something was said or intended to be said.

For example, there's a big difference between:

> He was a total jerk.

And:

> He was a total jerk. [Laughs.]

ONCE YOU'VE EDITED EVERYTHING AND BROUGHT IT TO THE CORRECT WORD COUNT, READ FOR FLOW. Flow is the key to a Q&A (and why a more conversational interview often works best). Did you cut anything that makes a question end abruptly and without context, making readers feel like they hit a wall? Does anything feel disjointed or stilted? Can the reader *tell* that it was edited down from a natural conversation? If so, you've got some more work to do.

DON'T THROW AWAY UNUSED PORTIONS OF THE INTERVIEW—ESPECIALLY IF THEY'RE GOOD. Editors will often purr like cats if you offer them the unused portions for an online exclusive, giving you a chance to run your full Q&A as conducted, and providing the editor with some Web exclusive content. You may even get a few more bucks, too.

THE REAL DEAL: THE JOURNALISTIC FEATURE

This feature is the meat and potatoes of many a publication. These pieces appear in large Sunday sections of newspapers and in magazines of all breeds. They're long and often heavy on research and interviews, and they take a deep look into a targeted topic.

BASIC STRUCTURE

Think of a journalistic feature as a newspaper article on steroids, with more room for style and alternate structures. But you don't have to write it so that your story can be chopped from the bottom up, inverted pyramid–style. Rather, you want to develop and deepen the piece as you go along. The key is to *tell a story.*

For the sake of classification, let's loosely categorize these articles into two types.

1. The Quintessential Journalistic Feature

While an editor will often dictate the structure, many journalistic features follow a basic approach: lede and introduction, followed by subheaded sections, ending with a recap and a kick quote. Because you'll be dealing with multiple sources and multiple interviews and transcripts, subheads bring a natural flow and structure to the article for both you and your readers.

I tend to start such articles with a fascinating tidbit—preferably via a narrative story—that will draw the reader in, while also setting up the main hook of the article.

After that, I review my transcripts and begin to loosely outline the story into subheads, tackling the major themes of the piece and providing a line or two about what each section will contain. My outlines are sparse, and I don't always follow them; I prefer to let the piece lead me where it wants to go. But my outlines are invaluable in helping me to see the bigger picture, and they prevent me from wandering too far off the path and into a wooded thicket. Think of an outline as the bread crumbs that will help you find your way back, should you get lost.

On any given day you might find a broad outline scrawled on a sticky note near my computer that looks something like this.

THE RISE, FALL AND ARREST OF OSCAR BOYNTON

INTRO
Boynton taking tickets and smiling; police enter and haul him off; basic details of the case

SUBHEAD 1: BACKGROUND
Where it all began; who he is in a nutshell; recapping his past

SUBHEAD 2: THE CRIME
What he did; how he did it

SUBHEAD 3: THE ARREST AND TRIAL

SUBHEAD 4: WHAT'S NEXT

Each section should ideally read as a mini-article within the larger piece—they should all have a beginning, middle, and end, and set up a good transition for the next subhead to follow.

In journalistic features, it's also good form (and a common writerly parlor trick) to employ the same circular structure discussed earlier to your overall article. Doing so will give your story a sense of unity and completion in readers' minds.

2. The Breakout-Style Feature

The other type of journalistic feature worth mentioning is this form, in which you begin with an introduction setting up the piece and then follow it with "breakouts." For example, an outline for such a piece would look like this:

"THE MOST NOTORIOUS CRIMINALS OF TOLEDO, PAST AND PRESENT"

INTRODUCTION: With Oscar Boynton's salacious acts making headlines, we decided to take a look back at Toledo's most notorious cons and criminals.

Breakout 1: Boynton

Breakout 2: Roger McCormack, seafood thief

Breakout 3: Detroit Tony

Breakout 4: Strangler Smith

Each mini-breakout would stand on its own, serving as a small profile of the subject described. They would not have to correlate or transition to one another, because they are presented in a "roundup" format. These types of pieces cover the gamut—from roundups of "5 Notable Scientists of the Year" to "The 10 Travel Destinations You Must See Before You Die."

Also worth mentioning here is what's known as "Dewar's Profiles." The first time an editor asked me to write an article using the Dewar's Profile format, I was confused—I'd never heard of it. Eventually I tracked it down to a vintage ad campaign Dewar's Scotch ran, beginning sometime near the early 1970s. The format, should you ever be asked to write in the style, simply translates to this familiar setup.

Home:
Age:
Profession:
Hobbies:
Last Book Read:
Quote:
Etc. Etc.

Now let's forget scotch-infused writing for a moment and take a look at a basic journalistic feature that, with hope, will bring some of the structure discussed above to life.

E-BOOKS: TAKE 2

Published in the November/December 2008 issue of Writer's Digest

At the dawn of the new millennium, the future was rising on a promising digital horizon. The Dow Jones, riding the dot-com wave, reached its highest peak. AOL and Time Warner struck up a behemoth billionaire partnership. Eyeing his own craft, horror maestro Stephen King had an idea to usher writers into the brave new century.

It was both revolutionary and risqué, and King's website said it had a chance to become big publishing's worst nightmare. In *The New York Times*, King even likened himself to an anchovy pizza; he was an experimental meal for the masses, and if people liked what they tasted, they might search for more and jumpstart a movement. The big news? E-books were emerging, and King was going to self-publish his work *The Plant* online. The story—appropriately, about a menacing plant that ravages a publishing house—would come out in serial form, which King would write as long as readers sent him a buck or two after they downloaded each chapter. If readers paid for 75 percent of their downloads, King would finish the story; if all went well, a model would be on the table that could bring higher profits to established authors and offer new writers a chance to be read without having to jump through the publishing world's hoops.

Throughout the industry, e-books were a growing force of unknown potential. Time Warner dreamed up a digital imprint, iPublish.com, and Random House broke ground with its own, AtRandom. Clunky and limited e-readers arrived on the market. Quickly, though, it became apparent that something was wrong with e-books: iPublish.com and AtRandom closed up shop in late 2001, lesser players filed for bankruptcy, and King quit nurturing his wily *Plant* to focus on other projects as paying readers tapered off.

Of course, with the debut of Amazon's Kindle, it's apparent that digitized content is back for a thriving round two. Writers considering the plunge from page to e-paper are left wondering: Is the groundswell really here to stay this time?

Industry veteran Bob Sacks, president and publisher of Precision Media Group, believes the answer is yes. "E-books are the future—exclamation point—for many reasons," Sacks says. "There was a point eight years ago in which they started and crashed. That's not going to happen this time. We've passed the point of no return."

Digital Domination

If you're a literary technophobe, the numbers can be frightening: According to the Association of American Publishers, e-books accounted for $7.3 million in estimated net sales in 2002. In 2005, $43.8 million. In 2007, $67.2 million. That's a 55.7 percent growth rate since 2002.

"Of course that's still only accounting for a very small portion of the market," says association Director of Digital Policy Ed McCoyd. "But you're seeing more publishers bringing out their front-list titles as both print and electronic editions." At the 2008 BookExpo America, the industry's massive trade fair, Amazon.com founder and Chief Executive Officer Jeff Bezos made a revelation. Since the Kindle e-reader launched in late 2007, books for the device had already managed to snag more than 6 percent of Amazon's sales. Light, wirelessly connected to a store in the sky and stocked with nearly all *New York Times* bestsellers—in addition to top newspapers, magazines and blogs—the Kindle is at the forefront of the e-book resurgence.

One reason e-books are finally taking off is superior technology—namely an e-paper display that mimics the printed page. "The idea was just as good eight years ago, but the actual reading experience wasn't good," Sacks says. "E-paper is the next huge leap." He predicts the devices will advance to color displays in a few years, before losing their hard-shell cases and morphing into audio-video-capable displays that can be folded or rolled, by about 2015 or 2020. (The Readius, a pocket e-reader with a flexible screen, is set for a United States launch in early 2009.) As Sacks says, "The Kindle is nothing more than the Model T of e-books."

Sacks and other industry pros say the future of the e-book movement isn't so much in the hands of publishers as it is readers: They'll fully embrace e-books when the ideal device debuts, be it from Sony, Amazon or (thus far mum) Apple. As opposed to 2000, experts say the time is finally right: New generations are completely comfortable reading on screen, people are more accustomed to mobile devices, the availability of content is better, and the public is focused on environmental sustainability. After all, "the words aren't less important if you read them on a screen than on a dead tree," Sacks says. "Bits and bytes don't fill up landfills."

As for the broad publishing world, Jeff Gomez, author of *Print Is Dead*, says the industry is trying to find a balance that works for everyone—readers, writers, agents, retailers and publishers. For some readers, Gomez likens the transition to the movement from vinyl records to CDs and MP3s. Nothing beats vinyl for some people, just like others won't ever give up printed books. But future generations raised online won't even understand all the fuss about e-books topping their print counterparts.

When it comes to a digital domination countdown, Gomez says to look around. Everyone is talking about the future, but major changes are happening now, most notably in the media. In the last year alone, *The New York Times* lost circulation and shrunk its page size. Microsoft CEO Steve Ballmer told *The Washington Post* that print newspapers and magazines would be completely gone in a decade. Mogul Rupert Murdoch, meanwhile, gave it a more optimistic lifespan of at least 20 years.

Andrew Savikas, director of publishing technology at O'Reilly Media, says execs see a future for e-books, but everyone is uncertain how big the market really is. He adds that publishers such as Harlequin have been innovative at delivering short-form book content on mobile devices, and players in the religion genre have been pioneers by creating a model that measures demand for out-of-print titles and digitally produces them when a critical mass has been reached.

Overall, though, Savikas says many publishers are missing the point. "There's too much of trying to replicate the print experience electronically," he says. "That misses the opportunity to take full advantage of what a digital environment offers." He says it could be as simple as hyperlinking text—and learning to do so automatically—that will make a big difference in giving the content a desirable advantage over traditional forms.

Does all this mean your treasured tomes—and your hopes of getting published old school—will disappear into cyberspace? Well, not totally. Books and magazines will always be around, Savikas and Sacks say, but they'll appeal to a more select crowd, becoming a collector's item.

At Academy Chicago Publishers, a small press that produces about 16 new titles every year, Vice President and Editor Jordan Miller says academics and students will likely substitute e-books for the gigantic volumes they lug around, but he doesn't know if people will enjoy reading novels in a digital format.

"Things could change," he says. "God knows they've changed enormously in the last decade."

While Miller acknowledged that he'd sell e-books if they brought in a profit, he says it will be the major publishing houses that will gravitate more toward digital content. Meanwhile, he believes small publishers might keep traditional books alive for future generations.

Golden Age or Era of Peril?

Terrified? Take a breath. Many industry vets think a digitized future will be a positive thing for writers. In fact, it might just be a great time to be a writer. Gomez says that when his first book came out in the mid-1990s, there was little he could do to drum up interest, and he had to rely on the media to write reviews and his publisher to spend marketing dollars. Nowadays, though, blogs, podcasts and social networking sites are free (or inexpensive) ways to reach a vast audience.

Gomez believes the revolution also will lead to more "wired" authors. He likens the transition to when sound was first introduced in movies; actors who couldn't adapt got left behind, as will writers who are reluctant to go digital. Overall, Gomez says the system could lead to more exposure—and more writers getting read—and the upsides outweigh any negatives. "Print being dead has nothing to do with either content, stories or ideas being dead," he says. "Writers—and readers—are very much alive."

Savikas also views the e-world as a boon for writers. "It's a tremendous way to no longer have to rely on the hope that your manuscript gets read," he says. "It's almost a golden age to be a writer because you have a tremendous opportunity to connect with an audience without needing someone else." This doesn't mean, however, that the traditional role of publishers—finding and fostering talented authors—will dissipate. After all, on-demand publishing and user-generated content have been around for years, Savikas says. But Sacks says self-publishing can take on new prominence with e-books—it's entrepreneurial for new writers to strike out on their own, and if they can get their work to enough people, they have the potential to go viral.

One area where Sacks sees potential change for publishers, though, is the traditional pricing model. He says the next development could be a cable TV-style subscription system in which readers pay for a package offering them newspapers, magazines and books (O'Reilly's Safari Books Online already has subscriptions for access to its e-cache). Which raises the question: Will writers see more money from e-book sales? For Sacks, it's the familiar crux. "Most writers, like most actors, are underpaid," he says. "Those lucky waiters who get noticed get the million dollar contract, while the guy who's next to him—who's probably just as good—doesn't. Some real talent will get noticed and some will go unnoticed."

While chatter abounds about how infrequently books are read in the modern age, McCoyd says e-books have the potential to grow the industry as younger people, lovers of all things digital, might be more inclined to read for pleasure. And, authors might also see an end to certain royalty dilemmas. As McCoyd points out, writers often believe they are due substantial royalties when publishers distribute many of their books, but instead they receive a financial blow when they're returned. E-books could allow for simple sales tracking and more accurate numbers.

Paul Aiken, executive director of The Authors Guild, takes a "wait-and-see" stance on whether or not e-books will be beneficial to writers. When it comes to digital media, Aiken warns that often a single player gets early control and winds up taking home the majority of the profits, as with digital music and Apple's iTunes. He says Amazon is building up its e-book library, and once it's in place, such dominant systems are hard to dislodge (Amazon did not respond to multiple inquiries for this article). "It's an interesting but also perilous time in the industry," Aiken says. "If this goes wrong, it could drain a lot of money from authors and publishers. Whatever promise the new media has could all be taken by one company, leaving authors and publishers to scrap over the money that remains." Aiken also says the market is already open through print-on-demand services, and while e-media could lower prices for consumers, it's not likely to generate a huge number of sales for titles that couldn't find a home in traditional publishing.

Sacks—who identifies himself as the industry's biggest curmudgeon—is actually optimistic about the future. "I think this is a great opportunity for creativity. It's truly the democratization of knowledge. It's what Gutenberg accomplished when he invented the moveable type and the printing press: People could afford to read. It's the same concept, but a hundred times more powerful."

Revenge of *The Plant*

So are e-books the future? In the end, it may come down to the opinion of the man on the street, the reader in the moment; you know, the kind who browses bookstores—online or in the real world—on a Sunday morning. At Joseph-Beth Booksellers in Cincinnati, Ryan Goldschmidt says he thinks e-books probably are the future. "It would make me sad, though, if we got rid of books all together," he says. Will he read e-books? "I'll probably be forced to."

Perhaps it's best to consult Stephen King, the man who helped launch an e-book revolution almost a decade ago. Questioned on his website whether his experiment *The Plant*—which, by the way, made a reported $463,832 in profit—will ever be finished, his reply is ominous, subtle and appropriate in the current debate.

"Time will tell."

TIPS

When writing in the journalistic feature format the following tips will help you organize:

ISOLATE YOUR BEST MATERIAL EARLY. When I've completed my transcripts and research, I'll pull it all together into one superdocument. Then, I'll read through everything and highlight the best of the best—facts and figures essential to the story, must-have quotes, and so on. Look for the info that is truly telling of your subject matter and necessary for the piece to be fully told. Doing this before you begin writing gives your subconscious a good guiding light, and eventually you'll find yourself plowing through the page without having to stop and look back through your notes every twenty seconds.

IF POSSIBLE, TRY TO CORRAL YOUR SOURCES WHEN YOU HAVE A LOT OF THEM. When you ping-pong between sources in your articles, it confuses the reader (especially if you introduce a source early on and then reintroduce him 2,000 words later using his last name only). Instead, as much as possible, I try to introduce a source, give him or her the spotlight, and then move on. And if I do have to reintroduce the source later, I'll try to include a few clues as to who the person is, based on his or her appearance earlier in the text. (For example, "Dugan, who opposes the sewer tax ...")

BECAUSE YOU'LL PROBABLY BE DEALING WITH A FAIR AMOUNT OF WORDAGE (1,500–5,000 WORDS, AND SOMETIMES MORE), EXERCISE CONSISTENCY. One of the biggest hurdles of writing long is losing your voice—starting the piece in one mood, going to sleep, and picking it up in a completely different mood the next day. The reader can tell when a writer does this. For that reason, it's always a good idea to reread the last 500 words of your piece before you begin the next writing session. Doing so will get you acclimated to the tone and style you already set and will prevent a lot of editing later.

PLAYING OFF PERSONALITY: THE PROFILE

With a profile, your objective is startlingly simple. You're answering one question for readers: *Who is this person?*

Of course, the focus of the story may be about something the person has recently done, an accomplishment, a failure, and so on, but your key objective is to answer that question, whether the person is famous, up-and-coming, or spectacularly average. That involves the individual's personality, backstory, the good and bad things she or he has done. That involves what this person *plans* to do in the future. And on and on.

Think of your article as a Polaroid of this person, at this moment in time. Let the colors be accurate and true, and the photo of excellent composition. Let it be an accurate memory in the album of a publication, a time capsule, a mini-biography, stylishly told.

BASIC STRUCTURE

The profile can be a relentlessly creative form. Here's the most bare-bones classic structure:

- Use a compelling lede.[3] I like to begin with a story—ideally, a narrative that I can carry throughout the piece—to draw the reader immediately into an interaction with the subject.
- Include the hook of the piece—why this person is worth examining at length—as early as possible. What has she done that is newsworthy, extraordinary, or terrifying? Include it up front, even if it's just a hint at what's to come. You don't have back-of-the-book cover copy to brief your readers on what's to follow, so give them a hint.
- Then jump back. Recap the person's past, often beginning with childhood and advancing forward.

---

3 Beginning to sense a pattern here?

- Cover the middle, followed by the present.
- Cover the future.
- Throughout, focus on the lens through which your editor would like the subject examined. For example, if I were writing about a writer for WD, I'd focus heavily on her writing process, her path to becoming a writer, and so on. If I were writing a piece for a travel magazine, I'd focus on the subject's path toward being a great adventurer, his exploits, and so on. If I were writing for a coin collector magazine, I'd focus on her collection, where she finds her pieces, her style, and so on.
- Wrap it up, and circle back to the start if possible.

The basic structure aside, you may have any number of other ideas for framing your subject. Don't be afraid to try them. I've written profiles that intersperse present-tense scenes with past-tense scenes. I've read great profiles that took place entirely within a single scene, start to finish. I've read profiles told in list form. If you find an alternate structure that you believe works, run it by your editor, and go for it. I rally around experimentation. After all, nobody says that you get only one shot. If you don't like what you've written, you can simply rewrite it.

All of that being said, here's a profile that didn't break the mold because it didn't need to. Instead it follows a simple basic structure.

THE ONCE AND FUTURE KING

Joe Hill set out to prove that you don't have to be the son of the most famous writer on the planet to be heir to the horror throne. But it just so happens he's both.

Published in the July/August 2013 Issue of Writer's Digest

One day, a funny thing happened: An unknown, frustrated writer named Joe Hill got an envelope in the mail.

A small one.

He'd been sending his short stories to *The Atlantic* for a while now, and thought he was getting close to breaking in. The rejection letters usually came in big envelopes containing his manuscript, but this one was different: It was small. Like, say, something you'd mail a check in.

Hill was married at the time, and he ducked into a pay phone to call his wife.

"I said, 'I'm so excited, I'm so excited, I think I just sold a story to *The Atlantic*—I'm going to rip the letter open and I'm going to read it to you right now—"

She said she was so proud, so excited, it was wonderful—

"—And I ripped the letter open, and it was a form rejection," he says. "And scribbled on the bottom was, 'Sorry, we lost your manuscript.'"

Hill erupts in a laugh.

"I was like, What the hell am I doing this for? I'm so sick of it."

Hill had been keeping a secret for years: He'd been writing under a pen name. His surname is actually King.

And his father, Stephen, is widely considered to be the most well-known writer alive.

Creative types sometimes wax and wane about whether writers are made or born.

Sometimes, it would seem, they're both.

■ ■ ■

Joe Hill was born Joseph Hillstrom King in 1972, two years before his father released his first book, *Carrie*, and nine years before his mother, Tabitha King, released her debut novel, *Small World*. He'd come home from school to find his dad working in his office, and his mom banging away on her IBM typewriter.

"It just kind of seemed like the most natural thing in the world to go up to my room and play make-believe for an hour on the assumption that eventually you'd get paid for it," he says.

As a kid, alongside his older sister, Naomi King (now a Unitarian Universalist minister), and his younger brother, Owen King (now a literary writer whose debut novel, *Double Feature*, came out in March), he lived storytelling.

"It sounds really Victorian, but when we sat around the dinner table, our conversation was all about books," Hill says. "After dinner we would go into the living room, and then instead of turning on the TV, we would pass a book around and read it."

After all, he adds, this was Bangor, Maine—there were only three TV channels.

It was natural, then, that Hill started writing on a steady basis when he was 12. He estimates that by the time he was 14, he'd set a daily goal of seven pages, which he could sometimes pull off in 45 minutes. At 14 (!) he wrote his first novel, *Midnight Eats*—a story about a school with a satanic dean ... and a cafeteria that (literally) serves up students who'd found him out. Even as a high-school freshman, Hill says he had a feel for his future genre of choice.

But in his mind, that genre already belonged to his by-then famous father. So when Hill entered the writing program at Vassar College, he made two decisions: to avoid the horror and fantasy genres, and to drop his last name from his byline. His reasoning for the latter was this: He was "deeply afraid" that a publisher would see a way to make a quick buck off of him, and it would result in a bad book with his name on it. He wanted a career of doing what he loved, not a fling.

"[Readers] may buy your first book because you're the son of someone who's famous," he says, "but if the book's no good, they won't buy the second one."

So Joseph Hillstrom King became Joe Hill. And in time, the pen name gave Hill an essential dose of freedom. He realized he could play in whatever genre he wanted.

Under his real name, he says he might have been judged harshly for writing horror and fantasy, stories sometimes not far off from the sort of stuff his dad wrote—but as it stood, no one knew who Joe Hill was. No one cared.

He produced a lot of stories. Around 1995, he queried literary agent Mickey Choate with a novel Choate describes as short and very dark, "but more literary than horror or dark fantasy." Choate took a chance on him without knowing his true identity, and the two never met in person—which was probably a good thing, given that Hill is a dead ringer for a young Stephen King (they even sound remarkably alike).

But ultimately, publishers far and wide rejected Hill's manuscripts. When his agent couldn't sell a certain fantasy novel Hill was fond of, Hill was heartbroken—"but in retrospect, [it] seems like it was a case of the pen name doing good work, because it wasn't good enough to sell on its own merits, and so better it didn't sell at all."

Hill's anonymous approach was not without exception in other arenas, though: After all, he says he needed to make a living, and so he did collaborate on a pair of screenplays with his brother under his real name. They sold one, but ultimately it wasn't produced.

As Hill was beginning to think that maybe he just didn't have a novel in him, he had a breakthrough in another realm: comic books. Marvel bought a SpiderMan story he'd written. (Had his fiction career not worked out, he says he'd have been happy as a staff writer at a comic book publisher.) He'd also been having some success publishing short stories. Hill would keep half a dozen in the mail at once so that when a rejection came through, it seemed as if he'd been only one-sixth rejected.

"I got to a point where I kind of felt like I'd rather sink with the ship than drop the pen name," he says. "I wanted to be able to say to my kid that I had a passion for something, I had a dream for something, and I stuck with it on my terms and made it work."

Eventually, his persistence paid off: A small publisher in England bought his short-story collection *20th Century Ghosts*, and released it in 2005. After almost a decade, Hill finally revealed his identity to his agent, and went on tour to support the book.

And as soon as he stepped foot onto the promotion circuit, people started to put it all together. The cat was beginning to creep out of the bag—but by then it didn't matter. The writing had come first. The pen name had done its job.

■ ■ ■

When you're writing about Joe Hill, a part of you longs to be able to relegate all mentions of Stephen King to a passing footnote. Here's why: Joe Hill can terrify. He can humor. He can sadden. He can shock. His characters are deep and vibrant, his plots mesmerizing, his prose genuine. Simply put, he's a damn good writer, and you feel like you're selling him short.

After *20th Century Ghosts*—which won several awards, including a Stoker for Best Fiction Collection—Hill released his first novel, *The New York Times* bestseller *HeartShaped Box*, in 2007. The tale earned Hill another Stoker, this time for Best First Novel. He followed it up with the popular Eisner Award–winning comic book series Locke & Key, and *Horns*, a 2010 horror novel with a romance component (which has been adapted into an upcoming film starring Daniel Radcliffe). His latest book, *NOS4A2* (sound it out), is a 700-page supernatural thriller about a mother, her son, and a man who abducts children and takes them to a terrifying place called "Christmasland." It was released in April to enthusiastic early reviews, and has been dubbed by Hill as his "Master's Thesis in Horror Writing."

For *NOS4A2*, Hill says he wanted to go big. He wanted to write something that spans many years, something with a lot of characters and subplots, and something truly scary. When he was younger, he says, he read a lot of great books in that vein—among them, his father's unforgettable clown classic, *It*.

"In some ways, *NOS4A2* is my rewrite of *It*," he says, laughing. "That kind of goes back to where we started this conversation, because I feel like most of the stories I write are partially a conversation with my dad, and my mom, and my brother and sister—that we're still having that same conversation we had around the dinner table."

As for being able to execute a novel of *NOS4A2*'s magnitude—or any great horror story, really—Hill says the genre is all about making readers care about someone, giving them a character they can root for, and then putting that person through the worst. He adds that when a piece of horror writing fails, it's often because the characters have transgressed into slasher-movie cutouts—characters you actually want Freddy Krueger to kill.

"If one of my characters is in danger, I want the reader to feel it and to care about what happens, not be hoping someone's head gets sliced off," he says. "I mean, I can match gore with the best of them ... but I do want the characters to be all there."

Moreover, he says bad genre writing too often involves characters acting out the expected emotional response: Something bad happens, someone cries. Something scary happens, someone runs.

"I don't think real people are actually like that," he says. "Sometimes something awful and sad happens to you and you feel blanked. It doesn't hit you until three days later."

Another way Hill suggests keeping a piece of fiction fresh: Drop the bear. Hill did a comic book adaptation of his story "The Cape" with his friend Jason Ciaramella. In the second issue, some police officers think a character murdered his girlfriend (which he did). The character, who has a cape that allows him to fly, soars to a zoo and gets a bear cub. The cops are in a convertible. He drops it in on them. Mayhem ensues.

"Since then, I've sort of joked that in every story, there has to be a moment where you drop the bear," he says. "It's sort of like the opposite of jumping the shark. You're looking for that moment where the readers' eyes pop a little, and you hit them with the punch they didn't see coming."

While Hill may keep his stories free of formula and cliché, he doesn't hide from genre labels. He's one of those refreshingly candid writers who calls it like it is, identifying his horror novels as, well, horror novels. ("It would make me crazy when I'd be reading an interview with some director who'd say, 'I don't really think of myself as a horror director.' And the movie he just directed is *Sorority Slasher Babes 7*. And I'm like, dude, no offense, you ain't [f-ing] Fellini.")

Hill doesn't see genre writers as a totally different species than "literary" writers. After all, he says, everything an author such as Neil Gaiman does with imaginative prose is at its core literary. On the flip side, he adds that many contemporary writers commonly thought of as "literary"—Jonathan Lethem, Michael Chabon, Karen Russell—are incorporating genre techniques into their work in wonderful ways, too.

"They're opening up the genre toolbox and playing with everything in it," he says. "It sort of returns genre to the larger literary family. It has helped make genre respectable again."

■ ■ ■

Given that his parents are who they are, you may be wondering: What's the best piece of writing advice they've ever given him? Hill says it's this: Finish the book.

Finish the book, regardless of how bad it is. You can make it better in a rewrite.

To that end, Hill describes himself as a big believer in habit. He usually begins his day by tapping in changes to the previous day's work, then writes five new pages, reads those pages over, and makes notes for the next day. Like his father, he works every day (weekends included) and writes organically—no outline. Which, seemingly, would be a good thing for father and son to have in common, given that they recently collaborated for the first time in print, co-authoring a couple of novellas. Readers of both father and son also will have undoubtedly noticed Hill's allusions to King's work in his own books—to the fictional town of Derry in *Horns*, to "the

Pennywise Circus" in *NOS4A2*—tiny Easter eggs for the "Constant Reader" that Hill says he's more comfortable featuring now than he would have been earlier.

Given that his parents are who they are, you may also be wondering: Which of Hill's books is their favorite?

Well, he says, always the most recent one, of course.

"They offer good advice, they have interesting things to say about [mine and Owen's] stories, but you have to remember that they're also parents. And so to a degree it's kind of like when your third-grader brings you a picture of an elephant, and [you] say, 'It's the best elephant ever!'"

As for what's next on Hill's plate, he's releasing new issues of Locke & Key, working on a novel titled *The Fireman*, and planning a TV pilot. He also still reads a lot—"I am like a 72-year-old man in a 40-year-old's body"—and spends a lot of time with his three sons.

When asked about what he wants to accomplish in his career before all is said and done, he pauses for a moment. Ultimately, the job of the day, he says, is to just write one solid scene. When you have one, you write another. When you have a stack, you have a short story or novel.

"I think for now I'm just paying attention to what I can see in my headlights. I'm not worrying about what's beyond them. One of these lines you hear a lot is, Live like it's your last day on earth! That's a really terrible piece of advice for a writer." He laughs. "You kind of have to live instead like you're immortal. You know, there's no rush to finish the book. It'll get done when it gets done. You sort of put off the idea that there's gonna be an end."

■ ■ ■

So: Are writers made or born?

While an author profile that fails to mention Hill's background is inherently incomplete—a crime of omission for the simple fact that storytelling is in his blood—fiction that fails to do so isn't. A story speaks for itself.

So forget writers being made or born. Perhaps a more meaningful question is: Do you like the book you just read?

Good stories, like Joe Hill's name, stand perfectly alone.

TIPS

When writing a profile keep in mind the following:

BEFORE THE INTERVIEW, READ EVERYTHING YOU CAN ON YOUR SUBJECT. Find out how she has been covered, in which outlets, and so on. What hasn't she ever been asked before? How can you shed new light on this subject, rather than merely rehashing the same profile that has been written about her before? Are there new questions you could ask, or a new structure you could employ to provide fresh insight on a well-covered subject? Gobble up everything you can, and then head in a new direction.

DON'T FORGET THAT YOU'RE TELLING A STORY. Sure, what you're writing might break down to be a miniature biography, but you need to employ all the tactics of storytelling to do it justice. Put the reader in scene as much as you can. (And don't forget that you can re-create scenes based on deep interviews with your subjects, as I sought to do in the introduction about Hill's *Atlantic* check.)

FOCUS ON *MOMENTS* AS MUCH AS YOU CAN. Coinciding with the tip above, try to isolate the truly cathartic moments in your source's life. Yes, they could be moments of the life-changing sort—but they don't have to be. Moments, both large and small, are ripe with telling detail. Consider film sequences that have impacted you. Yes, Luke Skywalker in Bespin Cloud City, with Darth Vader hovering over him, learning of his family lineage, is a hell of a moment. But on the flip side, if you've seen any of Wes Anderson's films, you'll know that the simplest moments set to music and slowed down can also have a hair-raising power—say, the scene in *The Royal Tenenbaums* where Margot Tenenbaum picks up Richie on the Green Line Bus, set to Nico's "These Days." Be open to bringing to life moments of all sizes in your stories.

CHOOSE YOUR POINT OF VIEW CAREFULLY. Would the story benefit more if you wrote it in third person (a more detached approach, using *he* and *she* pronouns), or first person (in which you inject yourself as the narrator of the piece, using *I* and *me*)? Most profiles utilize third person and remove the writer from the situation—and an editor may very well mandate that approach. But stories can sometimes benefit from a first-person narrator. Let's say you had to endure a crazy hunt to track down a subject who is a known recluse. The search for the person blended with the subsequent interview may make for a more enthralling—and telling—story than the interview alone. (A great deal of light could be shed on the subject if readers found out you had to cross four countries, endure a shipwreck, and crawl through a cave in order to find this person.) First-person point of view can allow for a more direct, intimate, and honest portrayal—and make for an overall better read.[4]

When deciding which POV to use, I do a rough mental outline of first- and third-person versions in my mind and select the one I feel will come together the strongest and offer readers the best experience possible. Either that, or I run it past my editor and ask her opinion.

INCLUDE AS MUCH TELLING DETAIL AS YOU CAN. An old professor of mine, Mike Redmond, advised us: "Brand of the beer, name of the dog." It's perhaps the most useful writing advice I've ever been given. It seems like a minute addition to an article, but sprinkling your piece with *real* detail adds that final missing dimension of authenticity and brings the piece to vibrant life for readers. For instance, was your subject drinking "soda"—or a Coca-Cola from Kroger, an organic soda from Whole Foods, or a Big-K six-pack from the dollar store? Was he drinking "vodka"—or Popov from a plastic bottle or a $120 handle of Grey Goose? Did she pet her "dog," or did she pet her Papillon/Chihuahua mix, Impi, or her frothing German shepherd, Death Knell? Don't underestimate the impact such seemingly benign details can have.

CHOOSE THE RIGHT QUOTES. This is important in all articles but especially in profiles. When you can feature only a limited amount of words from a subject's mouth, you have to make sure they're the ones that most strongly and authentically reflect her personality and pattern

---

4 Not long ago, I finished journalist Dave Cullen's nonfiction book *Columbine*. It was an excellent read, written over ten years and filled with mind-bogglingly good reportage, but a few passages threw me off throughout the book. Cullen would occasionally write things like "a journalist was present, and ..." Later, in the endnotes, Cullen reveals that he was in fact that journalist in the room. ... So why not just write *I*? Sure, a first-person appearance in an otherwise third-person book can feel inconsistent, and at times, jarring. But why not call a spade a spade?

of speech. In other words, if a source is joking around and being funny for 95 percent of the interview, you don't want to select an array of bland, superserious duds.

EXPLORE A THEME. Think deeply about your source before and after the interview. Ponder her endlessly. What major themes do the source and the conversation bring to mind that you could potentially explore in your piece to give it a heftier layer of depth? For the Joe Hill piece, I struggled with the Stephen King/Tabitha King element. I didn't want to diminish Hill's own talent and achievements by focusing on his famous parents (especially since he had gone to such great lengths in his career to avoid the subject), but they *had* to be included, as this was a piece about a writer who came from two great writers.[5] Did he excel at the craft because of the way he was raised? Was it merely in his genes? Nepotism could be eliminated, since he concealed his literary pedigree. So, for me, rather than dodge around it, that struggle became the focus of the piece—and tied back to a heavily recurring question in the art of writing: *Are writers made or born?* Once I'd locked that down, it was just a matter of telling Hill's story within that framework, which I used to explain Hill as a person and shed a degree of insight on his story.

TALK TO OTHERS. This may seem like hypocritical advice from a guy who just showed you a profile featuring only one other source. But generally you want to talk to an array of sources who know your subject—both friends and enemies—to develop a good, objective picture of your subject (regardless of whether you publish these insights). For the Hill piece, I talked to others but chose to keep the story tightly focused on Hill, mostly because he had the best insights, and I didn't want to junk the story up with redundant info. (I also didn't interview Stephen King for the reason listed in the previous bullet point.) Talking to others can give you great (highly quotable) perspective on your subject—and often provide deeper insights that will help you shape the questions for your primary source.

---

5 And the editor mandated that the Kings be mentioned, which made it an easier decision.

DECIDE ON SUBHEADS. I generally break things up with subheads. But sometimes I feel my transitions (and, usually, an asterisk) are enough. As Hunter S. Thompson said, "Not a wasted word. This has been a main point to my literary thinking all my life." While Thompson may have been guilty of drinking a wee bit too much and disregarding his own advice from time to time, I agree that the fewer words needed to get your point across, the better. No need to clutter a piece with unnecessary subheads. Let your inner scribe guide you.

■ ■ ■

Overall this chapter has been a brief (emphasis on brief!) overview of some of the key elements of typical structures in these forms. Entire books have been written on each of these structures, and I encourage you to check them out—or, with your newfound knowledge of the cornerstones, go it alone and develop your own voice and style. (For article types I have not included here—reviews, essays, travel pieces—log on to writersdigest.com/essential-guide-to-freelance-writing for a selection of pieces I have curated from writers who are masters of these forms.)

Overall the best thing you can do in your development as a writer is read every article you can get your hands on. Read widely, and read deeply. "The boys in the basement," as Stephen King calls the neurons firing behind the scenes, will pick up the forms and styles you like, and they'll get to work internalizing them and shaping your abilities in advance of your next writing session.

And as with all rules, many of those listed in this chapter can, of course, be broken. It just takes a damn good writer to do it.

So do it.

CHAPTER 8

THE MEN AND WOMEN BEHIND THE CURTAIN

"Creativity is allowing yourself to make mistakes. Art is knowing which ones to keep."
—SCOTT ADAMS

"Think of and look at your work as though it were done by your enemy. If you look at it to admire it, you are lost."
—SAMUEL BUTLER

"Newspaper editors are men who separate the wheat from the chaff, and then print the chaff."
—ADLAI E. STEVENSON

Finally: You researched a great topic and pitched it to an editor, got it accepted, and wrote it up. One last barrier remains between you and the prize of publication: submission.

A PREFLIGHT SUBMISSION CHECKLIST

Before rocketing a tin can full of people into the clouds, pilots do something amazingly simple to reduce the daunting set of complexities before them: They tick items off a checklist.

Sure, writing is less high stakes than safely transporting the Johnston family from Cleveland to Orlando. But if you take your craft seriously and want to excel at it—and do so in the quickest and most efficient way possible—then you need to make sure you're covering all your bases before you send any article to an editor.

As a writer, I mentally run through the following checklist before I turn in a piece. As an editor, this is what's going to make me trust your work once I'm on board.

It's easy to overlook the simple details, especially when you're moving fast. So before you turn in any piece, check off the following for the sake of your editors, fact-checkers, and, most important, your readers.

- **REREAD YOUR ORIGINAL QUERY, THE ASSIGNMENT, THE CONTRACT, AND/OR ANY CORRESPONDENCE YOU MAY HAVE HAD WITH YOUR EDITOR.** Does your piece contain everything discussed? Is the focus on point? Is there anything you accidentally left out? If you have, go back and tweak the piece so that it covers all the bases. *For bonus miles:* Reply in-line. In other words, keep every communication you have with your editor in the original e-mail thread pertaining to a particular story. That way, everything is in one place, and both of you can easily review the conversation as necessary.
- **FORMAT YOUR STORY IN THE PUBLICATION OR WEBSITE'S STYLE (NO MATTER HOW MUCH YOU MAY HATE IT).** *For bonus miles:* Ask to check out the publication's style guide before writing your article. The editor's inner nerd will glow with admiration and joy.

- **MAKE SURE ALL YOUR PROPER NOUNS ARE SPELLED AND CAPITALIZED CORRECTLY.** This includes source names, organizations, products, places, etc. Get these details wrong (and you'd be amazed at how many people do), and your editor will break out in a cold sweat and look around to make sure he's near an exit row. *For bonus miles:* No bonus miles shall be awarded at this level! Details are details, and you've got to nail them.

- **FACT-CHECK YOUR PIECE.** And I mean really go through it, top to bottom. Question everything. Verify everything. You don't want your editor to break down in tears because the great story you turned in is only 25 percent true—and it's about to go to press. *For bonus miles:* Do as *National Geographic* does. When I turn in pieces to *National Geographic Kids*, the publication requires that writers cite every single fact in the story. I do so in Track Changes in Microsoft Word. Think citations to links and books, and references to the origin of certain quotes. It's time-consuming, but it's worth it. Not only does it make an editor's life easier but it also gives you a layer of confidence that the work you've produced is truly solid. It also is likely to win you future assignments. For more on fact-checking, see the "Fact-Checking Checklist" in the Appendix.

- **INCLUDE A SOURCE LIST AT THE END OF YOUR STORY.** This is simple enough: Just list the names of everyone quoted, their titles, and their e-mail addresses or phone numbers. Editors can use this to verify information as needed. *For bonus miles:* Include mailing addresses for your sources. That way, an editor won't have to bug you later if she sends complimentary copies to sources as standard practice.

- **DOUBLE-CHECK THE QUOTES FEATURED IN THE STORY.** You don't ever want anyone to accuse you of misquoting them, so quickly check your recording and/or notes to make sure you're spot-on. *For bonus miles:* Include a transcript of the interviews you conducted, even if the publication hasn't asked for it. It doesn't have to be polished and print ready, just a resource for the editor to verify quotes, understand context, or pull additional material, if needed, for something like a Q&A. When people do this for me, it's the equivalent of the free wine you get on transatlantic flights: delightful.

- **READ YOUR FINAL DRAFT AS AN OUTSIDER.** By now you've probably lost objectivity for the piece. So disconnect for an afternoon, and then go back through the article with a faux-fresh eye. Ask yourself: If you were a reader, what questions would you ask? What's missing in the narrative? What doesn't make sense or requires further explanation? These are the questions your editor will be asking—and they may require time-consuming edits if you don't tackle them now. *For bonus miles:* Some writers I know read their work aloud because they feel it helps them come at it fresh. Don't hesitate to call in the trusted eye of a friend, either.[1]

- **MAKE SURE THAT IF YOU WERE ASKED TO PROVIDE PHOTOS OR ARTWORK, THEY'RE ATTACHED AND PROPERLY CREDITED.** *For bonus miles:* Consider suggesting captions. (I hate writing captions!)

- **INCLUDE AN UPDATED BIO.** An editor will likely be asking for it anyway, so get the jump on her and include it with your submission. *For bonus miles:* Provide two versions—a short one- or two-sentence version for the end of the article, and a longer one (about 65 words or so) for possible use on the Contributors page, should the editor want to feature you.

Overall, in my humble, nonexpert opinion, the essence of being a good pilot is doing your job well enough that your passengers aren't staring up at the ceiling, wondering if the oxygen masks are about to deploy. Go through this checklist when you're ready to turn in your article, and you'll save your editor the panic of scrambling around the cabin in search of a parachute.

All systems go?

Go.

---

[1] When we got married, my poor wife should have read the fine print on the marriage license mandating that she'll always be my trusted number-one beta reader. For better or worse!

TIME TO SUBMIT

Now, finally, something easy: sending in the finished[2] article!

When I file pieces, I usually tap out something akin to the following.

> SUBJECT LINE: Oscar Boynton Profile
>
> Dear Jessie,
> I hope all is well your way.
> Attached, please find the Oscar Boynton piece, plus a document of all relevant interview transcripts. All facts are cited in the Track Changes of the main article.
> Please don't hesitate to give me a shout if you have any questions.
>
> Many thanks for the assignment, and all my best,
> Zac
> [phone number]

Simple and straightforward. No need to overthink it, though if you have any details an editor should know about, now is the time to include them. (For instance, "You'll note that I only ended up utilizing four subheads in the piece, versus the five that we had discussed. I did this because …")

After the editor confirms receipt, you're in the clear for now—but be aware that it's not the end.

Here's a little secret about editors, one that bugs them as much as it bugs writers: Turnaround times tend to be wildly inconsistent.[3] For the magazines I've worked on, I generally set deadlines to fall around the time the previous issue is wrapping up and due to the printer. If all goes well, I can change gears immediately and work on the next batch of articles … but if all *doesn't* go well, and the production of the issue gets held up, I may not be able to get to the writer's article for a couple of weeks, leaving her to wonder what the heck is going on, and why the heck I requested it so early if I wasn't going to be able to get to it for another couple of weeks.

---

2 For now, until an editor whines about something and makes you change it.

3 This applies to turning in an article early, too. She'll definitely admire your ability to crank out a piece and be thankful it came in before deadline (it'll make her look good at the weekly staff meeting), but since she already has a time slot budgeted to edit it, she won't likely be able to take a look at it until the actual deadline.

For editors, the early request is a security blanket. If everything goes smoothly, they want to be able to jump straight to the next article. But it just doesn't always happen that way.

For every issue of my magazines, I set up a tracker that lists every story in the issue. It has a series of check boxes to document where each article is in the editorial process.

For instance, the checklist for the Boynton article might look like this.

[ ] Assigned
[ ] Article in
[ ] Art in
[ ] Article to design
[ ] First edit
[ ] Second edit
[ ] Paid
[ ] Fact check
[ ] Spell check
[ ] Final read
[ ] Signed off

When the editor is dealing with an issue consisting of twenty-plus articles, just marking those first two check boxes is a huge step. When it comes down to it, how fast an editor responds depends on how everything else is going in the process. (And, often, other factors, such as if another story set for the issue fell through and the editor needs a quick replacement—in which case he will usually stress the urgency up front, set a quick deadline, and then get back to you with uncharacteristic lightning speed.)

But the editor will eventually respond, and often it will take the form of one of the following:

- **"BEAUTIFUL PIECE."** It's perfect as is, you nailed the assignment, and, aside from the regular editing that is standard for every piece, no further action is required on your part. (This is the one I want, as both a writer and an editor! But it's rarer than you would think.)
- **"WE NEED A FEW TWEAKS."** The basics of the article are all in place, but the editor may need you to tweak the lede to make it better, add a stronger kick at the end, add some transitions, clarify

a few points in the article, etc. Ninety percent of all articles I edit tend to fall into this category.

- **"WE NEED A REWRITE."** The article either didn't deliver on the initial query, fell seriously short, is not well written, or other elements are way off base. While somewhat rare, this does happen. I've been guilty of writing an article or two that was off base, and though I hate to admit it, the rewrite I executed was always the better piece. And from the editor's viewpoint, trust me, we hate having to convey this news as much as you hate to receive it. We want all pieces to fall into the "beautiful piece" category.

The originating editor—the person who assigned you the piece—will serve as your main contact throughout the editing process. Once you and the editor have worked back and forth to produce a good piece, the rest of the editorial team[4] will generally give the piece an edit or a copyedit as well. That may result in a few additional questions from your editor on points of clarification, but from that point on, the work will generally be minimal, and all you'll have to do is sit around and watch the mailbox for your check while the editor dives in, gets things on the page, and gets everything prepped for print.

HOW TO WORK WITH EDITORS

Let's acknowledge the obvious: Editors can be divas. If I don't find a two-liter of premium coffee, ten fine-point red Sharpies, and a bowl of three thousand orange Reese's Pieces waiting at my desk when I get to work in the morning, I pretty much lose it.

That being said, it's not too hard to please such bratty creatures when you know the basics. Having worked on both sides of the fence, I've drawn up a list of best practices for working with editors, no M&M sorting required. (That's an intern's job.)

---

4 There are three basic types of editing: *developmental editing*, in which an editor really digs into the piece, from the structure to the overall feel; *copyediting*, which involves grammar, flow, consistency, and the minutiae of line-by-line work; and *proofreading*, which involves a last look at a "proof" of the story as it's set to print, and catching any errors within it. All three have overlaps, and their definitions can change publication by publication, but those are the three essential levels.

1. DON'T EVER THINK OF EDITORS AS DEITIES.

Leave that to them. Instead think of editors as creatives on the same level as you, working both sides of a mutual coin. Convey your thoughts to an editor. Converse with an editor. Work *with* the editor on the article. Be polite and friendly and open to the editorial process. We're all striving for the same end result: a damn good story. The editor will have the final say on how it publishes, of course, but a writer is a partner in the process, not merely a low-level tool to fill pages. Writers need editors—but too often people forget that editors need writers, too.

2. DON'T TAKE EDITING PERSONALLY.

As an editor and a writer, you would think it's easy for me to be edited. It's not. As writers, we have ego. We have vision. We *know* how the story would read best (or at least we think we do). I'd be lying if I didn't admit that I still get pissed off about certain edits. The trick is to let yourself be pissed off only for about five minutes (in which time frame you avoid all social media, telephone calls, and e-mail) and then to sit down and make a rational decision about whether you would like to pursue contesting a certain edit or want to leave it be and save your battles for another day.

As an editor, my philosophy is "do no harm." That being said, each editor I know has a different style and different approach, and whether she has a light hand or a heavy hand varies. Some editors totally rewrite articles. Others barely touch them. Some editors will pop in conclusions or intros. Others will ask the writer to do so or will suggest phrases. Some editors will cut entire paragraphs or sections of an article on a whim. Others will nervously break out in a cold sweat at the thought of changing even a single word.

This is all to say, be prepared for a variety of approaches and styles. It's a wildly inconsistent professional standard for a bunch whose professional lexicon involves the word *consistency* no fewer than twenty times daily.

In my opinion, the good editor is the one who works alongside a writer but isn't afraid to dig into a piece to tune it up. The good editor is one whose definition of good editing isn't just putting something in her own voice and style.

Regardless of how she accomplishes it, an editor's goal is to use her knowledge of the written form, and particularly her own magazine, to create a story that readers will find value in.

Know that an edit is never personal. It's just a matter of doing one's job. That being said ...

3. PICK YOUR BATTLES, AND THEN PICK YOUR MARKETS ACCORDINGLY.

If you don't like your editor or think he's a bad editor based on your experience working together on an article, you'll know not to work with him again. You may love an editor's magazine but despise his process. Ask yourself: Is it worth it?[5]

4. DON'T GET MAD IF THE EDITOR GOES SLOW.

I realize I keep circling back to this, and who knows, I may subconsciously be trying to cover my own hide or issue some equally truant apologies. But it's important for writers to understand that delays are inherent to all publications. Before I started working as a magazine editor, I would stress out from the moment I sent in a story until I heard back, which could take weeks. Was it my writing—was it bad? Was it so bad that it merited weeks of contemplation and reworking until the editor was finally ready to lay the bad news on me? Not so. The reality is that, simply, publications have been doing more with smaller staffs. Whereas once an editor could sit high on a throne and edit manuscripts with a quill pen day in and day out, that is far from the case these days. A big part of that is growing digital responsibilities. At *Print*, for example, I write articles for the magazine, solicit pieces from freelancers, blog, edit blog posts, edit the entire magazine, fact-check, send con-

---

5 Even if the answer is no, fear not. Editors change on a daily basis in the publishing industry, so it's more of a waiting game than anything.

tracts, file invoices, create storyboard lineups for the magazine, manage associate editors, manage and market entire competitions, help program the massive HOW Design Live Conference, edit e-books, and occasionally serve a janitorial role of taking boxes out to the dumpster. I love it. I love every moment of it (even taking out the boxes—hello, sunlight!). And I want you to know that the lag is not because of your piece. It's just the way the game is played these days.[6]

5. REALIZE THAT EACH STORY IS, ESSENTIALLY, A BIT OF A TEST.

When editors work with writers (and when writers work with editors), each interaction builds a fragment of a larger overall impression, from the query to the contract negotiation to the questions that come up during the writing process to the time the story hits our in-boxes and the editor begins to work with the writer, right up through to the publication of the piece. Throughout the process, if you're easy to work with and produce solid work on a consistent basis, more assignments will come.

And this is, at its heart, the ultimate goal of freelancing: the Relationship. As I said in the query chapter, you don't want to keep starting at square one with a publication, slush piles and all. Rather, you want to build a mutually beneficial relationship. You want to earn your spot as a publication's trusted go-to writer. Then, when you pitch strong ideas, since the publication has worked with you before, they'll know they can trust you to pull it off. And, moreover, they'll come to *you* to write on assignment. At that point, a full-fledged relationship is established, and we've proven to each other that we can make mighty fine articles together.

As an editor, I crave these types of relationships. With looming deadlines and the need to produce the best magazines I can produce, having trusted partners in crime is truly essential. What keeps me up at night? The fear of losing our best writers. Without them, the magazine wouldn't be the magazine, especially if the writer has a strong voice readers have come to know and love.

Financially, when a writer has a relationship like this with a publication, he may be put on retainer, too, which means stable income—a vital treat for freelancers.

---

6 Which may explain why you'll get random e-mails at 2 A.M. on a Sunday.

CHAPTER 9

MOSTLY NOT BORING BUSINESS BASICS

"The freelance writer is a man who is paid per piece or per word or perhaps."
—ROBERT BENCHLEY

"When I say work I only mean writing. Everything else is just odd jobs."
—MARGARET LAURENCE

"Why did you become a journalist?"

"Better than working for a living."
—LESLIE COCKBURN, *BAGHDAD SOLITAIRE*

And now, for the least fun topic of all: business talk! I promise to keep the math simple and the windedness short. Remember: This stuff may be a pain in the ass, but it'll keep the lights on and the water running and, with hope, buy you a yacht someday. Here are the basics.

PAYDAY!

In freelance writing, payment is all over the place. It's sometimes great; it's sometimes ridiculously bad. But sometimes the hilariously crappy checks are what lead to bigger and better things, while a one-time, great-paying assignment may get you nowhere in the long run. Again, choose your assignments wisely. (As I'm writing this book, I'm also working on a magazine article for 25 cents per word—coming off of an assignment that paid $2 per word—simply because the subject is fun and I think it'll be a good clip.)

A number of factors play into what your payment will be. Generally, this is how it works: The bigger the publication, the better the pay. The more wide-reaching the publication, the better the pay. The more your experience, the better the pay. The more specialized the topic, the better the pay. The more extensive the research and reporting, the better the pay. The more you've written for the publication, the better the pay.

Ultimately you'll find that your payment will depend on what the publication has available in its budget. When I'm planning an issue for *Print*, I'll first look at the amount of editorial pages I have to play with (all the pages that aren't set aside for advertising). Then I'll look at my set budget for the issue (which we negotiate with our publisher once a year). Then I factor in our regular per-word pay rate, which influences both how many articles I can acquire and how long each article will be.

I pay writers as much as I can afford to give them. Editors often find themselves in a "use it or lose it" budget scenario, where they *want* to spend their full budgets so that those budgets aren't lowered the next year. If a pay rate extended to you is truly awful, the publication might just be pinching pennies—but often the cheapness goes far up the food chain, and the editor is merely attempting to do the best she can with the small budget she was given.

One publication might pay a standard rate of, say, 25 cents per word. Another might have a much higher standard rate and, often, tiers of payment—for example, 30 cents per word for front-of-the-book content, 60 cents for features, 75 cents for a feature writer who has been working for the publication for years, and $2 for a well-known writer who contributes on occasion.

It's worth noting that publications often have different payment models. I tend to like per-word payment structures best because you get the most accurate representation of your compensation. The dilemma for many writers is that they don't take into account or know the *time* involved in different types of assignments. A 1,000-word opinion column is going to be a hell of a lot easier to bang out than a 1,000-word investigative piece. So if an editor offered me 40 cents per word for a 1,000-word column, I'd take it, but I'd narrow my eyes at a 40-cents-per-word pay rate for the investigative piece. As a writer, begin to recognize your strengths and to know which articles you find the most rewarding and which you're best at—and thus which you're the fastest at producing.

Some publications pay per assignment. For example, they'll offer $600 for a column or $1,500 per feature. (In those cases, since I'm fond of per-word rates as a standard, I'll take the word count and divide the pay by the words to determine my fee—and my level of interest.)

Some assignments pay per hour, but you'll find that setups like this most often apply to the business world, PR/advertising, editing, etc.

When it comes to writing for magazines, newspapers, websites, and so on, be weary of the editor who asks, "How much do you charge?" That puts the power in his court and begins a psychological game in which you don't want to lowball yourself but you also don't want to price yourself out of the market.

In those situations, I would ask, "How much do you generally pay writers for this type of assignment?" Or "What do you have in your budget?"

The goal is to get as much as you possibly can and to work within the publication's budget. They know how much they can afford to pay, and an honest editor will pay a writer as much as he can while staying within his budget.

Every year, *Writer's Market* surveys a number of professional organizations to determine the high, low, and average payments for various writing endeavors. Here are a few highlights. While this book focuses on editorial freelancing, I've included some advertising and PR items here to give an idea of the take across various disciplines.

This, with hope, will serve as a good starting point for knowing the ins and outs of compensation.

MAGAZINES AND TRADE JOURNALS			
	HIGH	**LOW**	**AVERAGE**
Arts reviews	$1.25/word	12 cents/word	63 cents/word
Book reviews	$1.50/word	20 cents/word	73 cents/word
Consumer magazine columns	$2.50/word	37 cents/word	$1.13/word
Consumer front-of-book articles	$850 project total	$320 project total	$550 project total
Ghostwritten articles[1]	$10/word	65 cents/word	$2.50/word
Trade journal feature articles	$3/word	20 cents/word	$1.20/word
Medical/scientific writing	$2/word	25 cents/word	$1.12/word
NEWSPAPERS			
	HIGH	**LOW**	**AVERAGE**
Arts reviews	60 cents/word	6 cents/word	36 cents/word
Book reviews	60 cents/word	25 cents/word	44 cents/word
Unsyndicated columns	$1/word	38 cents/word	50 cents/word
Feature writing	$1.60/word	10 cents/word	59 cents/word
OTHER FIELDS			
	HIGH	**LOW**	**AVERAGE**
Advertising copywriting	$3/word	30 cents/word	$1.57/word
Catalog copywriting	$350/item	$30/item	$116/item
Press/news releases	$2/word or $750/page	50 cents/word or $150 page	$1.20/word or $348/page
Brochures, booklets, flyers	$2.50/word or $800 page	35 cents/word or $50/page	$1.21/word or $341/page
Corporate periodicals	$3/word	$1/word	$1.71/word
Newsletters	$5/word or $1,250/page	$1/word or $150 page	$2.31/word or $514/page

1 Higher paying because you're doing all the work and receiving none of the credit.

Technical writing	$160/hour	$30/hour	$80/hour
Government agency writing/ editing	$1.25/word	25 cents/word	75 cents/word

CONTRACT BASICS

First things first: When an editor asks you to write a piece, make sure you will, in fact, be getting a contract for it. Without one, you're at the mercy of your editor on everything from rights to word count, and you have no recourse should the editor decide to kill the piece, close up shop, or, well, not pay you.

Contracts are awful and no one wants to deal with them, but we have to—and, in fact, understanding the terms of a contract is vital to making sure you don't get a raw deal. To begin, after your article pitch has been accepted, you'll generally receive an e-mail or phone call along these lines.

> Dear Zac,
>
> We would like to commission this piece as pitched.[2] We can offer you 40 cents per word for the piece, set to run at 2,000 words. We would be looking at a deadline of 11/15.
>
> Please let me know if you accept, and I'll get an official contract sent your way.
>
> All my best,
> Tom
> --
> Editor

From here, you can either accept immediately or work back and forth with the editor on the deadline until you reach an agreement. If you feel the fee is too low, you can also negotiate an increase by offering a logical argument.

> Tom,
> Thanks so much. I'm thrilled you're interested in the piece and would love to do it. The deadline and word count sound good, but

---

2 A rarity! In general, editors try to twist and contort your idea to their nefarious whims.

might you be able to go any higher on the fee? Given that I'll be talking to nearly twenty-five sources for the article, it will involve an extra allotment of time, especially to get it in by 11/15.

Many thanks in advance for your time and consideration, Tom.

Regards,
Zac

Or:

Dear Tom,
Thanks so much. I'm thrilled you're interested in the piece. The deadline and word count sound good, but might you be able to go any higher on the fee, or offer reimbursement for the phone calls I'll be making? Because the article will involve a high number of international phone calls, I worry that the cost of the phone bills may rise higher than the sum of the article.

Many thanks in advance for your time and consideration, Tom.

Zac

Or:

Tom, quit being a cheapass! Good words cost good money, and you know that.

Zac[3]

Tom's budget may be exhausted, and he may very well tell you so or explain that the fee is the magazine's standard rate, etc. If you really feel it's not worth it, you can bail—but understand that you may never get an assignment with that publication again. (Of course, if the fee is too low, you might not *want* to approach Tom ever again.)

In my experience, you may get a few more dimes if you push back, but it likely won't be a game-changing increase. One quickly gets the sense that there's not a whole lot of wiggle room.

But assuming you do go forward, it's contract time.

Some contracts are simple. Others are like phone books and include appendices and various clauses that sign your life and work away.

---

3 Which would quickly be followed by an apology and a note about how my e-mail account was hacked.

Let's take a look at a sample contract covering the essentials. As with most legalese, there is always a simpler translation, which I'll attempt to provide after every section.

Magazine	
Writer's name	
Writer's address	
Writer's tax ID (SSN) #	
Assignment	
Length	
Photo/art requirements	
Deadline	
Compensation	
Kill fee[4]	
Expenses	
Biographical info for attribution	
E-mail address	
Phone	

Zachary Petit Publications, ("ZPP" or "Publisher") makes, and Writer accepts, the assignment described above on the terms and conditions set forth in this Agreement.

1. DELIVERY/ACCEPTANCE

Writer agrees to submit, no later than the Submission Deadline noted above (unless Publisher agrees in writing to an extension), the completed manuscript in a mutually agreed upon digital text file format together with, for any persons depicted in accompanying photographs or illustrations, identification and background facts sufficient to permit the writing of appropriate, accurate captions and accompanying text. The completed manuscript, together with any supporting photographs, art, tables, or sidebars (each to be delivered in a format and medium acceptable to the Publisher), shall constitute the Work. Writer shall also obtain and provide, at Writer's sole expense, written permission for use of third-party material and appropriate model/subject releases for any accompanying photographs, each to be in a form provided by or acceptable to the Publisher.

Acceptance by Publisher of the Work will be by specific written notice. Requests for changes, approval of draft materials, favorable

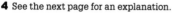

4 See the next page for an explanation.

or unfavorable comments, and other matters in communications to
the Writer will not be deemed conditional acceptance, acceptance
or rejection by Publisher.

In a nutshell: You must abide by your deadline, e-mail the file, and provide credits and permissions for everything you'll be sending in. (Some
publications include fines for every day the submission is late.)

It's worth noting here that there are two ways to get paid:

1. Payment on Publication (POP)
2. Payment on Acceptance

What you want is "Payment on Acceptance," which means that when
the editor signs off on the piece (per the terms indicated in the contract), he also asks the accounting department to cut you a check. "Payment on Publication" is where the waters get murky and a writer can
become trapped in the quicksand of BS. I've heard horror stories about
writers selling their work on POP contracts and then the publication
holds the story for a few years, or indefinitely—meaning no payment.
Newer publications and financially unstable publications are most often the culprits here. In general, I would never write for a publication
that offers these terms. (Once the baton of the article has been successfully passed from writer to editor, your work is done. If a publication
wants to sit on or hold an article, it should be at their financial disad-
vantage, not yours.)

2. CANCELLATION WITHOUT CAUSE/KILL FEE

Publisher reserves the right to cancel the assignment without cause,
in which event Publisher shall pay, and Writer agrees to accept in
full satisfaction, the Kill Fee noted above.

This one is a biggie. Seeing anything containing the words "kill,"
"dead," etc., in a contract is not something most new writers are comfortable with. But a kill fee is actually a good thing, and something you
want to see in your contract. Basically a kill fee is a level of insurance
for both the writer and the editor. If an editor decides to cancel an article for any reason—it may be that it's bad and simply unfixable, that
the publication is canceling the thematic issue the article was set to appear in, that the publication is closing, etc.—then he can enact the kill
fee, which pays the writer a percentage of the original agreed-upon fee.

I generally issue kill fees at around 25 percent. So, for instance, if WD contracts me to write an article that pays $1,200, and I completely drop the ball and fall off the radar, the editor would cut me a check for $300 (and never talk to me again).

Having a kill fee in a contract lets the editor know that he won't be screwed should the writer totally botch the assignment, and it lets the writer know that just because a nitpicky diva editor doesn't like the piece, a portion of the work will still be compensated.

I should add here that I've only ever had to pay three, maybe four, kill fees in my time as an editor. Editors don't like paying kill fees. It means that they'll have a hole in their next issue that will need quickly filled, and that they'll be ponying up some dough for the privilege. Thus I always work with a writer to salvage articles and only have deemed them unsalvageable in a couple of instances. (Most of these situations involved writers who were difficult to work with or refused to make changes.) The other instance when I enacted a kill fee was after a magazine I worked for commissioned a year of a column shortly before finding out that they had to cut eight pages from every issue that year, resulting in the column being canceled and a year of kill fees paid.

3. GRANT OF RIGHTS

Exclusive Rights
Writer hereby grants and assigns to the Publisher the following exclusive rights in the Work:

- First North American Print Serial Rights;
- the perpetual, worldwide right to reproduce, display, and distribute the Work in digital, individually retrievable form via a website or database associated with the Magazine identified above

Nonexclusive Reuse Rights
Writer further grants and assigns to the Publisher the following additional, nonexclusive rights in the Work:

- the perpetual, worldwide right to repurpose and republish your work in other publications published or licensed by ZPP,

- the perpetual, worldwide right to license adaptation and translation of your work for republication in domestic and foreign distribution, and
- the perpetual, worldwide right to include, and license the inclusion of, your work in digital media and databases, in individually retrievable form or otherwise, and for electronic reproduction, display, and distribution by any means (whether now known or hereafter invented).

The grant of rights is a core element of a contract. It says, essentially, what you're giving up. Grants of rights can appear in different variations, the most distinct being "First Rights" vs. "All Rights." Ideally you want "First Rights"—meaning the publication has first dibs to publish what you've written. After publication, the rights revert back to you, the writer, and you can repackage or resell the piece elsewhere, post it on your website, sell it to an anthology, etc. With "All Rights," everything is not all right—the publication has eternal rights to your piece, to do with it what they will.

Going bullet by bullet, the second point in the previous excerpt just means that the publication has the right to put the piece on their website, etc., for as long as they'd like.

As for the nonexclusive rights, the first bullet means that the publication is allowed to reprint the piece in an anthology, collection, etc. Whether or not you'll be paid for it depends on the info in the following excerpt. The second bullet indicates that the publication can have it translated or adapted for foreign editions. The third (which can get tricky) is a blanket clause a publication uses to secure all digital rights for the future—the kicker is the "whether now known or hereafter invented." When e-books first emerged, publications were thrown into a tizzy because the contracts writers originally signed were specific to the print rights that existed at the time. Debate then emerged about who had the e-book rights. Clauses like this seek to clarify and strengthen the publisher's hold on the work for whatever might be invented in the future.

4. COMPENSATION

Provided that the manuscript and all other elements comprising the Work are delivered on time and are satisfactory to Publisher in both form and content, Publisher shall pay to Writer within 45 days of acceptance of the Work for publication, as a one-time fee, the Compensation specified above.

In the event Publisher reprints the Work in any of its books or other print magazines, Publisher shall pay to Writer an additional sum of 25% of the original Compensation for each such reprint upon publication of same. Writer shall bear his/her own expenses unless, and to the extent, reimbursement is authorized above. Any authorized reimbursement is limited to the Writer's reasonable and necessary costs, in accord with the Publisher's expense reimbursement policy, and conditioned upon acceptance of the Work for publication and the Writer's submission of receipts or other acceptable evidence of disbursement.

This section of the contract informs the writer when the check will be cut (in this case, forty-five days after acceptance). It goes on to add that if the company reprints the material in another of their publications (an anthology or annual collection, for instance) the writer will receive a fun-money check of 25 percent of the original fee. (Yay!) It also lays down the law that you're not allowed to recklessly rack up McDonald's charges (or any others) as you write the piece and then invoice them to the magazine.

5. RIGHT TO EDIT

Publisher reserves the right to make such editorial changes as are necessary to conform the manuscript to its house style and standard usage. Publisher agrees that in the event it determines that material, substantive changes to the manuscript are necessary or appropriate, Publisher will make reasonable efforts, time permitting, to contact and consult with the Writer and take into account the Writer's comments prior to publication of the Work as revised.

In other words, editors gonna edit. And they'll try to work with you so that everyone is happy (unless the deadline is in the next forty-five minutes).

6. ATTRIBUTION

Publisher shall include in each copy of the Work an attribution, in house style, based upon the biographical information set forth above.

The publisher promises to give credit where credit is due.

7. WRITER'S REPRESENTATIONS AND WARRANTIES

Writer warrants that, with respect to Writer's contributions to the Work: Writer is the sole and original author of the Work (excepting any material identified in the Work as third-party material) and has full power and authority to make the grant of rights set forth herein; Writer is not restricted by contract from entering into this Agreement or carrying out Writer's obligations hereunder; the Work contains no matter that is libelous, an invasion of privacy, or otherwise unlawful; the Work does not infringe upon any statutory copyright, common-law literary right, or proprietary right of any third party; Writer has used and will use all reasonable care in the creation, research, and preparation of the Work to ensure that all facts and statements in the Work are true and correct in all material respects; and no instruction, formula, direction, recipe, prescription, or other matter contained in the Work will cause injury or damage.

By signing the contract, you're verifying that no secret parties ghostwrote the piece for you, and that you have the rights to what you've written, which you're now handing over to the publication. Furthermore, you're doing due diligence and not providing anything that will get the publication sued.

8. INDEMNIFICATION

Writer will indemnify and hold Publisher harmless against all claims settled by Publisher or reduced to judgment, including all court costs and reasonable attorneys fees and expenses.

You'll find this in many contracts. Essentially it means that if the publication gets sued for what you've written, you'll be responsible for it—not the publication. Obviously many writers take umbrage with this and may seek to get it struck from a contract. (I do.) "All claims" is a bad thing—it not only means that you'll be responsible for ethical breaches (which you should be) but also that any Joe Schmo can sue you for something absurd. If you push back on a publisher regarding this line, mention that many publications no longer abide by this tenet and that it could infringe upon your ability to freely and truthfully report a story. Many resources about such contractual language can be found online.

9. NONCOMPETE

Writer agrees not to write, prepare, participate in, permit the use of the Writer's name in connection with, or be financially interested in any work on the same subject intended for publication within 90 days of the first scheduled publication date of the Work unless the Writer has obtained the prior written consent of the Publisher.

Basically, you can't take the subject of what you just wrote for a publication and sell it to one of their competitors the next day (unless, of course, it's your area of expertise and you're always going around hawking it, in which case you can negotiate this clause per the "prior written consent" above).

10. INDEPENDENT CONTRACTOR

Writer shall be an independent contractor for all services performed pursuant to this Agreement, and nothing herein shall be construed, by implication or otherwise, as creating an employer/employee, principal/agent, or co-venturer relationship between Publisher and Writer. Accordingly, no tax withholding shall be made from payments to Writer under the provisions of this Agreement. Notwithstanding the aforesaid, Publisher shall have the right to make such withholdings and report any payments made to Writer as required by law. Writer shall not be entitled to receive any employment benefits, including but not limited to vacation pay, sick leave, retirement benefits, Social Security, workers' compensation, disability, or unemployment benefits, offered to employees of Publisher.

You're a freelancer and not a staffer, and you'll be paid untaxed—meaning you'll have to pay the taxes you owe to Big Brother next April, lest he come after you. Moreover, the publication will be reporting what you were paid to the IRS so the IRS knows to come after you. And, finally, in case you were wondering, writing a front-of-the-book piece does not mean you'll get a 401(k) and two weeks of paid vacation.

11. MISCELLANEOUS

This Agreement represents the entire agreement of the parties with respect to the subject matter hereof and supersedes any prior or contemporaneous writings with respect thereto. Any changes to this Agreement must be made in writing and signed by all parties.

> Any dispute, controversy, or claim arising out of or relating to this Agreement, or the breach, termination, or invalidity thereof, shall be settled by arbitration by a single arbitrator under the Commercial Arbitration Rules/Expedited Procedures of the American Arbitration Association and judgment on the award rendered by the arbitrator may be entered in any court having jurisdiction thereof. This Agreement shall be binding on and inure to the benefit of the parties hereto and their respective successors and permitted assigns; provided however that, as this is an agreement for personal services involving a relationship of confidence and trust between Publisher and Writer, this Agreement, and any rights and obligations arising hereunder, may not be assigned, sold, pledged, or otherwise disposed of, in whole or in part, by Writer without Publisher's prior written consent and then only in accordance with such consent.

Such legalese basically amounts to the following: Break the rules, and we'll see you in court.

Reviewing a contract can be daunting. But realize that most of this language is not unlike the body armor worn by a street cop—there in case of an emergency, and otherwise just there, without incident, 99 percent of the time. If editors had their way, they wouldn't even use contracts—they're a pain in the ass to create, send, and file. But the lawyers call the shots, and they'd be suing the editors if someone sued the publication. So the contract stays.

The important thing is to ensure that your contract covers the needs of both writer and publisher—and doesn't put the ball unfairly into anyone's court or infringe unnecessarily upon your basic artistic and creative freedoms, not to mention your wallet.

So what do you do if you want something in your contract changed?

Start a dialogue. Explain what's bothering you, and inquire if anything can be done about it. Some editors will just say, "Sure," scratch off an offending clause, and then mail it back for you to sign. Others will flat out tell you they can't touch the contract lest a lawyer materialize to fire them.

Get a feel for your bearings, and engage in a polite, open dialogue about any issues you might have.

"CAN YOU SEND ME AN INVOICE?"

Well, can you? If you know the basics, it's simple. A publication needs an invoice to initiate the payment process and provide record of the transaction. They'll ask for it once they've formally accepted your article. When you draft your first invoice, save a template version that you can reuse every time. Basically an invoice includes the following:

- your full legal name (the name your check should be paid to, which may also be your business's name)
- your mailing address (where your check will arrive)
- your social security number or federal tax ID (this is needed for the accounting department, though the publication may already have it on file from the W9 they likely sent you to fill out)
- the date of the invoice (highly useful should your check not arrive within forty-five days from the time you submitted the invoice)
- the name of the project, how many words it was contracted at, and the fee (highly useful for jogging an editor's memory and, well, getting the right number on that check)
- an invoice number for follow-up (this can be anything—"ZP00001," for instance; develop your own system for easy accounting)

You could plop all that into a Word doc with no formatting and no frills and send it off. But on some weird psychological level, a nice-looking invoice denotes professionalism and makes you seem like you're running a top-notch business. Get into your editor's head. Templates can be found on many software programs and everywhere around the Web.

WAIT A SECOND ...

But what happens if the forty-five days pass and you still haven't seen hide nor hair of a check? You, my friend, are dealing with a delinquent client.

The first step is to reach out to your editor—calmly!—and just say that you're e-mailing to check on the status of the invoice. Stuff happens on the editorial end—even if it's just overlooking the invoice and lazily forgetting to submit it on time.

But what if your editor doesn't write back?

Try again. And then once more, if you don't get a response. At this point, you're still operating under the assumption that a simple mistake has been made. Who knows? The editor might be on vacation.

Still no response?

Let's kick it up a notch. Look on the masthead and go up a level. If your contact was an associate editor, go to the managing editor. If your contact was the managing editor, try the editor. Again, tread lightly, but get your point across.

> [date]
>
> Hi Mr. Bernaise,
> My name is Zachary Petit. I recently wrote a piece about Oscar Boynton for *The Daily Herald*. I haven't been able to get in touch with Roger Sherman regarding payment for the article, which I have not yet received.
>
> Might you be able to help me out, or point me in the right direction?
>
> Many thanks,
> Zac
>
> --
>
> Zachary Petit
> [phone]

Some will say that I'm being too lenient and not harsh enough. But remember: You catch more flies with honey, and all that. I'm still giving the editor the benefit of the doubt, in case my e-mail has been landing in a spam in-box or the check was mailed to the wrong place. After all, if your experience was good and it's a venue you'd like to keep writing for (assuming they, well, pay writers), it's not time to burn the bridge quite yet.

But let's say the publisher doesn't respond. The entire editorial staff has seemingly gone MIA. Before we get the matches out, let's first try the accounting department. Compose a polite message explaining the situation, the amount, the invoice number, and so on. Send it off. Cross your fingers.

Still nothing?

Flick the match. Screw the bridge. If it doesn't serve its purpose, then you don't want to be traveling on it anyway.

It's time for a demand letter.[5]

This is the last chance for the publication to pay you what's due. If they don't, everyone's headed to court. And this demand letter (along with your other correspondence) is what you'll happily show the judge.

First off, remain calm. State the facts. Don't get overly emotional. Moreover, be as concise in detail as you can. Provide names. Dates. Times.

I've never had to send one, but it might go a little something like this.

Oct. 1, 2015

Dear *Daily Herald* editor Roger Sherman, publisher Tom Bernaise and head of accounting Denise Reinhold,

On July 5, 2015, Roger Sherman contracted me to write a 2,000-word profile of local theater ticket-taker Oscar Boynton at a rate of .50 cents per word ($1,000 total). The article was turned in and formally accepted on July 20, 2015, and was published on July 28, 2015. Thirty-five business days after payment was due (per the publication's thirty-day payment terms), I contacted Roger Sherman via e-mail on September 5, 2015 to inquire about its status. I received no response. I followed up on September 10 and September 15, and received no response. Phone calls placed to Sherman were also not returned.

On September 20, I contacted Tom Bernaise via e-mail and telephone and received no response. On September 25 I contacted Denise Reinhold via e-mail and telephone and received no response.

This letter is to inform you that the payment of $1,000 for the article is now fifty-three business days overdue. If I do not receive full payment of $1,000 by Oct. 8, 2015, I will immediately begin pursuing legal remedies.

Regards,
Zachary Petit
[phone]
[email]

---

5 To prevent my own ass from landing in court, it's disclaimer time! This is shared wisdom, not "official legal advice."

Make copies—those will come in handy should you need to venture over to small claims court to recoup your grand. And finally, keep a record of when you sent the letter and track it, just in case the nefarious Roger Sherman claims he never received it.

KEEP YOUR EYES PEELED

I've never had to pen a demand letter (well, until now). And you shouldn't ever have to either. The key to avoiding such awfulness is to know which markets to avoid from the start.

Here are some warning signs that a market might be one you don't want to touch with a ten-foot pole. Learn to read the writing on the wall and to know what buzzwords should make you immediately suspicious.

"START-UP"

Recoil like a snake at the mention of working for a start-up. It might be good for a clip or to have some fun, but if you're in it for a paycheck, as my editor put it: "It's like entering a bear cave with steak strapped to your legs." Start-ups are notorious for not having adequate funding, for leaving writers hanging, for holding articles indefinitely, and, moreover, for going out of business.

"PAYMENT ON PUBLICATION"

I mentioned this a moment ago, but it's worth noting again here.[6] You have to immediately question *why* a publication would not pay on acceptance.

My friend, writer Linda Formichelli, once likened it to going out to a store to get a new suit. You wouldn't grab the suit, tell the clerk at the register that you'll send the store a check if you decide to wear it, and then head out the front door.

So why would a publication not pay on acceptance? Well, for one, they might not have enough money to cut the check right away (a bad

---

6 And I should add that while throughout this book I often generalize "publications" to mean any outlet for your work, here, we're talking "publications" in the most literal sense. Websites offering a "payment on publication" model are less of an issue because the "publication" happens almost instantaneously.

sign). ... And, who knows, if that ad they're hoping to get from McDonald's doesn't come through, they might not have the funds at all.

Moreover, as a writer, you don't know how long you're going to have to wait. (I've held some pieces, for one reason or another, for more than a year. While the writers of those pieces were likely—and understandably—annoyed, their fury would have been much greater had I also withheld their check.) Is it a weekly publication? Monthly? Bimonthly? Quarterly? All will affect when that check will finally hit your mailbox. So before you agree to such a contract, get the date—in writing—of when your article is set to publish.

PUBLICATIONS WITH A REPUTATION

If you'd like to pitch a new market that you've discovered, do a little background research first. Think of it as the requisite Google stalking you do before going on a date with someone. You don't want to find yourself in a bad relationship.

Moreover, writers are bad people to piss off. What we do is write. So if we get ripped off, there's a good chance we'll write about it. And a cursory Google search of your new market will often reveal any complaints that have been filed on the Web.

Also, don't hesitate to Google the name of your market with a "BBB" to see if anything comes up on the Better Business Bureau. You probably should drop by the "Bewares, Recommendations & Background Check" forum on Absolute Write (a fantastic website) to stay abreast of the latest bad business out there, as well.

ANYTHING ON CRAIGSLIST

There has been a rash of news stories lately about people being held up/beat up in parking lots because of predators and deals gone wrong on Craigslist. So it is with the writing services tab of the site. Like most things on Craigslist, from "massages" to $100 cars, there's more than meets the eye to a lot of posts. And Craigslist is where many the desperate freelancer goes to scrape the bottom of the barrel, to varying effect. Expect a lot of too-good-to-be-true offers promising you thousands every week for selling your words! Avoid them. Avoid princes from Nigeria who would like their life stories told in exchange for $1M USD. Avoid exciting new **START-UPS** offering $25 checks with Payment Upon Publication terms. Avoid trading your words for anything other than cash.

Sure, there are a few viable writing opportunities to be found from time to time.[7] But if you're really looking for a place with legitimate job postings, try Mediabistro, JournalismJobs.com (more for the newspaper crowd), Elance, and other resources, such as Career Builder or Ed 2010.

"TRIAL PERIOD"

Think of this market as one you would encounter walking down a city street late at night. "Hey, guy, come over here, I wanna show you somethin'," a man in a bowler hat and tattered coat would call from the depths of an alley.

These markets are skeezy. They're up to no good. And they're known for screwing over writers.

The basic ruse is that they're recruiting new writers for this or that, but first they want to see if you've got the chops, so rather than looking at clips like a normal publication would, they'd like to take you for the old test-drive. And the result is that you get taken. You write a bunch of articles for them for free, they publish them, and then they magically decide, *Well, this isn't working out! On to the next scribbler!* (This type of market is commonly found online.)

"GET YOUR FREE SAMPLE!"

Similar in scumbaggery and level of deceit, but slightly more merciful in scope, these publications will ask you to write a "sample" piece for them so they can determine if you're a good fit. And before you know it, you're looking at your piece online while simultaneously reading an e-mail that says you're not a good fit.

---

7 In fact, while working for a weekly newspaper, I once sought out columnists on Craigslist. But I did so because nobody at the paper would give me the money to post on JournalismJobs.com. And I did so fully realizing my ad was two clicks away from comprehensive listings of escorts in the area.

CONTENT MILLS

You didn't really expect me to get all the way through the book without hating on them one last time, did you?

THE TERRIBLE SUBJECT OF TAXES

For this nefarious topic, I was originally going to contact some tax experts and have them pen this part of the book. But then it hit me: Why hand the keys to the castle over to some suits and pantsuits whose words none of us will be able to understand anyway?

Let's go it alone. I'll cover the basics in the broadest sense, and in the easiest language, possible. (And I promise to have a tax expert look this over before it publishes so she can verify that I'm not going to get us all thrown in debtor's prison.)[8, 9]

Tax deductions can seem like a mystical world to writers. *Should you try to get them? Will you get called out by the IRS for trying to get them? Are you legitimate enough to declare yourself a bona fide independent business owner to curmudgeonly Uncle Sam?*

For too long I lived in fear of deducting anything. I figured I hadn't made enough money or earned my stripes as a full-blown freelancer, and would get called to the floor by the IRS if I listed my $80 recorder as a deduction.

So for years I stupidly lost money, and I missed out on a lot of legitimate deductions I could have deployed had I only known the most basic ropes of the game. As I'm writing this, it's tax season. And you bet your backside that next to my new iMac is a huge pile of receipts that I fully intend to write off.

---

8 With many thanks to the brilliant Eric Eggemeier and Corinne Tirone Eggemeier for subsequently looking this over and assuring me I *probably* won't land any of us in a Victor Hugo-style lockup.

9 High time for yet another reminder that this does not constitute formal legal advice—just the musings of another harmless writer.

THE FACTS OF LIFE

So this is what sucks: If you made at least $600 from any one client in the previous year, every January or February said client will send you a 1099—essentially a form stating how much, total, they paid you. They'll also be so kind as to send a copy to the government to further ensure that you pay your dues. As mentioned earlier, every check you received for freelance work was completely untaxed—meaning you now have to pay up.

As freelancers, we're taxed higher than your average bear. We don't have bighearted, generous employers throwing into Social Security on our behalf, and so because of our independence, we pay a higher premium. *We* are those employers. This is exactly why we want to accrue all the deductions we can to offset our higher taxes.

For purposes of classification, when you're an official employee of a company, you get a W2 every year stating your earnings and so on. As a freelancer, you have a whole other host of alphanumerically designated forms to deal with.

Rather than dealing with all the forms and rifling through a million pages with a pencil, I use the business edition of a tax software program, which is usually one step up from the basic model and costs a few bucks more, but is always worth it. The program will cover all of your essentials and walk you through the process so that even someone like me, who was highly encouraged to take more Algebra instead of stepping up to Calculus with everyone else in high school, finds the whole thing to be manageable and simple. The software will prompt you for the dollar amounts directly correlating to the line items on your government forms, help you determine your status as a freelancer, let you know what deductions or privileges you're eligible for, and so on. And here's the crucial part: It'll crunch all the data for you, tell you what you owe, and let you know if you're in audit territory.

In the year leading up to this excruciating game, take simple steps to ensure that you'll be ready when April 15 draws near. Every time you get a paycheck, set aside a percentage of it so that you won't take a financial gut shot in April. (Thirty percent of every check is a good amount to bury in your backyard.) Moreover, whenever you pay for anything that has *anything* to do with your freelance work, keep the receipt. Stash it in a folder, even if you're not sure you'll be able to use it. You'll be glad you did.

DEDUCTION TIME!

Now here's the burning question, and perhaps the only exciting thing in this entire section: What can you deduct? A lot. Let's dive in here.

YOUR HOME OFFICE. Think rent! Taxes! Repairs! The possibilities are endless if you set up a room in your house as your home office.

Debbie Downer says: Here's where things can get a wee bit tricky. You'll need to figure out the percentage of your home that you use as an office. (You can do so by dividing the square footage of your home vs. your office—simple math that even I'm capable of.) From there, you can deduct portions of your home office expenses as applied against your home.

COMPUTER. Gone are the days when a computer was a luxury item. Now the government recognizes that a writer needs much more than a pen, paper, and bottle of cheap gin to do her job.

Debbie Downer says: But, of course, the Minecraft game on your computer isn't going to look so good to the IRS, nor is your collection of meditative whale songs (unless you're a video game writer or a whale songwriter, I suppose). In other words, if you're deducting 100 percent of your computer, it should be 100-percent used for business only.

OFFICE SUPPLIES AND EQUIPMENT. Think digital recorders. An extra monitor for your computer. A mouse pad. Paper. Postage.

Debbie Downer says: Just don't go nuts. You don't want to build yourself a technological wonderland to the tune of $20,000 and make $23 in freelance income that year.

SOFTWARE. This makes the sucker punch of having to pay for a basic writing program that should have come with your computer in the first place a little less painful. (I'm looking at you, Microsoft Word.)

Debbie Downer says: Again, don't forget Big Brother. He's watching when you're using Microsoft Word to create a Little League batting order for your son's team.

PHONE AND INTERNET. Yes, you indeed need both to be able to function as a working writer today.

Debbie Downer says: But you're not doing business when you're calling Uncle Larry in Tampa to see if he can score you Disney World tickets at a discounted Florida resident rate. Or when you're blowing through gigabytes of data to download the latest Hollywood blockbuster. Remember: Keep track of percentages.

SUBSCRIPTIONS. How are you supposed to write for magazines if you don't get any? Now is the time. Also, this category could include memberships in professional writing organizations, online stylebooks, and things of that nature.

Debbie Downer says: But not membership to your local cat appreciation club. Unless you write for Catmondo!, *I suppose.*

WRITING CONFERENCES. Not only fun and great networking opportunities, but also highly deductible—including travel expenses!

Debbie Downer says: I have no objection here.

NECESSARY TOMES. Time to pick up that copy of *Writer's Market* I've been rambling about.

Debbie Downer says: Not all books qualify. For instance, you'll have to pay for that first-edition copy of Carrie *you've been lusting after. Just think of how good it would look on your bookshelf ...*

TRANSPORTATION AND TRAVEL—WITHIN REASON. Need to travel to meet with your editor about a big project? That can be deducted. As can mileage to a research site, a trip to interview sources, and so on.

Debbie Downer says: But you can't just go on a month-long journey to Belize to research an article you're flirting with pitching to an editor. Well, you could, I suppose, but I wouldn't advise it—unless you bring me back souvenirs.

BUSINESS MEETINGS. Go ahead. You know you want to have a glass of bourbon with your editor.

Debbie Downer says: Just don't take her on a trip to Belize—unless you both bring me back souvenirs.

WEBSITE AND OTHER PROMOTIONAL MATERIALS. While my website runs on WordPress, GoDaddy handles the hosting. But that doesn't mean I'm proud to be forking over a chunk of change every year to a company known for trashy Indianapolis 500 ads featuring Danica Patrick. This, like the Microsoft Word situation, softens the blow.

Debbie Downer says: If it bothers you so much, why don't you just switch Web hosting providers?

THE PROGRAM THAT DOES YOUR TAXES. This is divine, and probably my favorite item on the list.

Debbie Downer says: Rock on with your bad self.

There are lots of other things you could theoretically expense. But in all honesty, I'm not comfortable putting the more ludicrous ones here. I have friends who abuse the system to comical degrees, but I'm more reserved. The Clash taught me long ago what happens when you fight the law: The law tends to win.

THE HOBBY LOSS RULE

So maybe you're hesitant to file any deductions. Is your writing a hobby at this point, or a business? Turns out the government can actually help us a bit here.

The rule of thumb: If you strike freelance gold and come out in the black three years out of five, you're viewed as an official business. If you have lost money in three out of five years, you're more likely to be classified as a hobbyist, and the IRS may get all twitchy, thinking you're trying to get undue deductions by misclassifying something.

That being said, Uncle Sam is at least practical. He acknowledges that you likely won't be making a profit right out of the gate—and that you can file necessary deductions as you work yourself up to a point of profitability.

So make it rain with your words, and deduct away.

EINS

To go further down the business rabbit hole, how far should you go in legally formalizing your business dealings?

While that rabbit hole runs vast and deep, and is a question best left to an accountant, I would recommend getting an Employer Identification Number—a.k.a. an EIN. You can obtain one for free in minutes: All you have to do is log onto the IRS website, pull a name for your business out of a magician's hat (I went with "Writers Live Twice"), file your request, and magically secure your shiny new EIN. You can then use it in place of your Social Security number on W9s, which will not only make your business and services look more formal but will also better protect you from identity theft[10]—and allow you to do fancy things like open credit cards in your business's name (ever helpful when attempting to expense one's iMac).

PLAYING WITH UNCLE SAM

As freelancers, we're prime targets for suspicious auditors. For all they know, we're attempting to write off our dollhouse addiction by classifying it as a business rather than a hobby. My philosophy has always been to recoup what's due to me from the government—but to not get greedy. (And I'm not just saying this in fear that an auditor is reading this book, attempting to determine whether I'm a dollhouse hoarder or a dollhouse vendor.) I play *with* Uncle Sam rather than against him. Nothing will slow your writing career down faster than a nice, long stint in Sing Sing, where the shank-wielding locals don't take too kindly to white-collar criminals whose primary weapon is words.

If you're unsure about anything, just ask an accountant. It's always better to be safe and strategic than sorry.

---

10 If you're seeking peace of mind, I would not recommend walking through the offices of a publishing company, where you're likely to see stacks of contracts on an intern's desk, Social Security numbers and all.

CONCLUSION[1]

GETTING TO -30-

"Just write every day of your life. Read intensely. Then see what happens. Most of my friends who are put on that diet have very pleasant careers."

—RAY BRADBURY

"Keep a small can of WD-40 on your desk—away from any open flames—to remind yourself that if you don't write daily, you will get rusty."

—GEORGE SINGLETON

---

1 "-30-" is journalism-speak for the end of a story.

CONCLUSION

Throughout this book, we've covered the gamut, the A to Z of free-lancing: what freelancing is, how to find markets, what you can pitch those markets, how to pitch those markets, how to conduct interviews for the markets you've pitched, and how to write what you've pitched for those markets.

One final thing before we part.

As a writer or aspiring writer, you're likely tired of being bombard-ed with messages like: "YOU CAN BE A WRITER!" "ANYONE CAN DO IT!" "YOU COULD BE THE NEXT BESTSELLER!"

Such messages seem like a gross oversimplification of a wildly complex endeavor. Sure, it's easy to tweet that, but doing it? As we all know, it's a whole other ballgame.

I have an office in my basement, and I ran upstairs to get a cup of tea just a moment ago. "What are you doing now?" my wife asked me from the couch, thinking I was done with words for the evening.

"I'm going to write a conclusion to the freelance book really quick," I replied, and trotted down the long set of stairs to the computer.

Yes, those "You can be a writer!" messages are grating and, at times, demeaning. I hate to admit this, but there is a reason you hear them so often: They're true. All it takes is the will to trot down those steps to your computer.

Writing is a matter of putting in the time.[2] As has been said in many ways before, write a few words and you've got a sentence. Write a few more sentences and you've got a paragraph. Write a few more paragraphs and you've got an article or a chapter. Write a few more chapters and you've got a book.

Sure, that first article may be absolute shit, *but you'll have an article.* Whether you decide to fix it or write another one is up to you. But write more you will, and better you will get.[3]

All it takes to write is time, repetition, and trust in your instincts. If you're meant to do this, your instincts will guide you, and with time, editors, readers, and the rest of the crowd will notice.

To that end, don't forget why you came to the blank page in the first place. Especially after reading a book like this, you may feel

---

2 This book was written largely in hour-long stints after my nine-to-five job.

3 That came out sounding like Yoda. Sorry.

mired in a swamp of rules—rules dictating form, function, how to do this, how to do that.

Recognize them, but don't let them bog you down. Don't let them drown out the passion for the craft that initially drew you to it.

When you sit down at a blank page, sit down with a blank mind. *Just write.* Close your eyes, and do what you're hardwired to do. Feel the magic. Let it lead you where it will.

Afterward you can turn the logical side of your brain back on and assess what you've written, how you wrote it, why you wrote it, whom you wrote it for, and everything else discussed in the book. Just don't let it overtake the pure, raw euphoria of the craft. It is a sacred thing, and as long as you write, it should stay that way. I've let my craft turn into other things at various points in my life, and nothing has felt better than closing my eyes and getting back to why I started sitting down at the keyboard in the first place.

As we close, I'd like to offer the following, which a wise, old, grizzled reporter, editor, and teacher named Charles St. Cyr once wrote to me: "Journalism is an adventure. Enjoy the journey as best you can. How you manage your journey is your contribution to what journalism is or should be."

I'll leave it at that.

But not, of course, without annoying you one more time with the following:

Anyone can be a writer.

So be one.

APPENDIX

THE BEST STUFF THAT WOULDN'T FIT IN THE BOOK PROPER

SAMPLE QUERIES

As promised: more queries! If you're seeking a triple dose of inspiration or a recap of things done right, read on.

Here's one from writer Donald Vaughan, who shared this pitch that resulted in a commission from *Cat Fancy*. From the raw, striking lede to the transition into the core elements of what the article will include, Vaughan turns his personal story into a pitch that will undoubtedly benefit the publication's readers.

Ms. Debbie Phillips-Donaldson, Editor
Cat Fancy Magazine

Dear Debbie:

We buried Mai Ling, our Himalayan, today. She had a stroke yesterday morning, and we had her put to sleep at an emergency clinic late last night.

Dr. Frank Bandel, our veterinarian, told us that stroke is a common ailment in older cats, but that often they are able to throw it off and live many more years in near perfect health. He urged us to give Mai Ling a couple more days before making our final decision, but as the evening wore on, it became evident that she was slipping away. She quickly lost the use of her hind legs, was unresponsive to touch or voice, and completely blind. Even though she wasn't in apparent pain, it was clear that to keep her like that would be cruel, so we had her put down. It was a difficult but necessary decision.

Based on this experience, I would like to pitch a *Cat Fancy* feature on cats and stroke. I was amazed to find that the symptoms are very similar to that in humans—partial paralysis, loss of specific senses, catatonia, etc. The most intriguing aspect, however, is that small animals such as cats are often able to overcome what would result in lifelong disability—or death—in humans.

In this piece I would discuss how common stroke is among cats, traditional symptoms, common causes, which breeds are most susceptible, what owners can do to reduce risk (if anything), how cats respond physiologically to stroke, how they are able to throw it off and how owners can make life easier for a cat that has experienced a stroke. I would also discuss common ailments that can mimic the symptoms of stroke in cats, including hypoglycemia, diabetes and renal failure. My primary sources would be Dr. Frank Bendel, who saw Mai Ling; Dr. Andrew Faigen, director of For Cats Only in West Palm Beach, FL, and neurologist Dr. Julia Blackmore.

I hope you find this idea of interest, Debbie. It was extremely difficult losing Mai Ling—especially since we lost our Siamese, Mandy, just last year—but hopefully others can benefit from this experience. Should you wish to discuss this idea further, please don't hesitate to call me at [phone number].

Thank you for your time and consideration. I look forward to hearing from you.

Sincerely,
Don Vaughan

APPENDIX

This query, from author Craig Silverman to *Writer's Digest*, resulted in a commission for a front-of-the-book story. Note how Silverman establishes his credibility on the subject instantly, details what the piece will contain, and even explains how his piece will differ from a recent article we had published on the topic of accuracy. Moreover, he touches on the narrative elements of the piece, which gave me a chance to see how it would come together on the page and fit within the magazine.

Hello [Jessica Strawser, editor of *Writer's Digest*],

I'm a journalist and author based in Montreal. Jane Friedman passed along your e-mail address after I told her that I'd sent an article query to the general submission address at *Writer's Digest*. She suggested I send it along to you.

I'm the editor of Regret the Error (www.regrettheerror.com), the media errors and corrections website, and author of *Regret the Error: How Media Mistakes Pollute the Press and Imperil Free Speech* (Union Square Press/Penguin Group Canada). I also write a weekly column for Columbia Journalism Review and am a former columnist for *The Globe and Mail.* I have an idea for a first-person InkWell article. The story details how I came up with a new way to correct errors contained in my book. It also reveals the surprising amount of joy I experienced from publicizing my own mistakes. Call it the "Joy of Error." Every writer should experience it.

My book, which was just released in paperback, is about the history, cause and impact of media errors. I've spent over four years researching and blogging about the issue on my website, and my book won the 2008 Arthur Rowse Award for Press Criticism from the National Press Club in Washington. While writing the book I was confronted by an obvious challenge: How would I handle my own inevitable mistakes? I spend a good part of the work chiding newspapers for not offering proper corrections, so I needed to walk the talk. I needed to invent a new way to identify and correct book errors.

The system I came up with relies on free online tools that can be used by any author. It also helped me connect with readers and even generated a little bit of publicity. I'd like to share this with your readers. Here's what I did:

- Included a Statement of Accuracy at the beginning of the book. This brief section outlines the steps I took to fact-check the book. It also reveals the weaknesses of those steps and asks readers to help me discover factual errors. I informed readers that they could report errors using a form on the book's website (book.regrettheerror.com) or by mailing in a printed form contained at the back of the book. Finally, I told them they could read all of the book's corrections at my website.

- Created an Error Report form both online and in the back of the book. This form encourages readers to hold me accountable. To my knowledge, no book has ever included an error report form.
- Maintained an Online Corrections Page. The book's website houses all of my corrections. This has been done before, most notably by Seth Mnookin. But I took it a step further: Readers could sign up to receive corrections either by RSS feed or by e-mail. That way, they could come to my site once and then automatically receive the latest corrections either in their RSS reader or in-box.

In the end, I published 12 corrections to the book, 11 of which were the result of reader submissions. All of the errors are corrected in the paperback, and my new introduction gives credit to some of my error-spotting readers, bless their hearts.

Now, after the release of the paperback, I can't wait to see if readers will step up once again and help me correct more errors. I also hope this article will encourage other writers to embrace the concept of book corrections.

I believe this piece could work well in your front section, but I would also be eager to expand it into a larger essay that can provide more detail about The Joy of Error and Thrill of Correction. I can also produce sidebars that give step-by-step instructions for handling book corrections and preventing errors. (I realize you published a Tips piece about accuracy in the Feb. 2008 issue, but I have some useful advice that wasn't covered in the piece.)

I'd be happy to send you a copy of my book, and you can read some of my clips at www.craigsilverman.ca. I also encourage you to take a look at a recent op-ed I wrote for the Toronto Star: www.thestar.com/comment/article/556662 and read my CJR columns: www.cjr.org/regret_the_error. They relate to this topic.

I'm very excited about the possibility of sharing my experience and expertise with your readers, and would love to be a part of your magazine.

Best regards
Craig

And finally, this query, from writer Kerrie Flanagan to *Writer's Digest*, also resulted in a commission. This is one of those "who-the-hell-knew?" pitches, and she executes it perfectly. I had no idea Andrew McCarthy is now a travel writer, and so I was immediately intrigued—and knew our readers would be, too. Flanagan weaves in the great narrative of how McCarthy got into travel writing in the first place, makes the pitch, recaps her deep writing experience, and leaves it at that. I was reaching for the *Writer's Digest* checkbook soon after.

> Dear Zac,
>
> … Andrew McCarthy, best known for his roles in 1980s classics like *Pretty in Pink* and *Weekend at Bernie's*, is not one of those celebrities dabbling in writing; he is a writer who happens to be a celebrity. Since his first published article in *National Geographic Traveler* back in 2006 to the release of his best-selling memoir in 2012, McCarthy has and continues to show his talent as a writer.
>
> He is an editor-at-large at *National Geographic Traveler*, and his dozens of articles have been published in publications like *The New York Times*, *The Wall Street Journal*, *Travel + Leisure* and *National Geographic Adventure*. The Society of American Travel Writers named him their 2010 "Travel Journalist of the Year," and in 2011 he won their "Grand Award."
>
> Ten years prior to the publishing of his first article, he traveled the world and journaled about his experiences. He then began reading travel magazines and felt there was a lack of depth in many of the stories. He set up an appointment to meet with the editor of *National Geographic Traveler* and told him he wanted to write for the magazine. When the editor said, "You're an actor," McCarthy replied with, "Yes, but I know how to tell a story." After a year of e-mails and badgering, the editor finally agreed and sent McCarthy on assignment to Ireland.
>
> McCarthy says he has become successful as a travel writer for two reasons. "First, travel profoundly affected my life and is the undercurrent in everything I write. And secondly, I approach my writing from a story-first point of view."
>
> I am proposing an article profiling Andrew McCarthy. He is an incredible writer who doesn't just tell readers about the places he is visiting; he takes them along with him using vivid descriptions, authentic dialogue, compelling storylines and a willingness to show his vulnerability. Through interviewing him, I will find out

how he is able to achieve this depth in his writing, how he is able to find good stories, what his writing process is, other writers he admires, the challenges he faces with writing and how he is able to find continued success.

I am the director of Northern Colorado Writers and a freelance writer. Over the past decade I have published 130+ articles in national and regional publications and enjoyed two years as a contributing editor for *Journey* magazine. I have articles in the 2011 *Guide to Literary Agents*, as well as the 2012, 2013 and the upcoming 2014 *Writer's Market*. I am a frequent contributor for WOW! Women on Writing, the author of the children's book *Cornelius Comma Saves the Day* and five of my stories have been published in various Chicken Soup for the Soul books.

I look forward to talking with you more about this article,
Kerrie

--

Kerrie Flanagan
Director: Northern Colorado Writers
Freelance Writer
[address]
[phone]
www.KerrieFlanagan.com

FACT-CHECKING CHECKLIST

Everyone hates fact-checking, but it's a necessary evil. To help out WD's associate editors, I created this brief checklist:

- Are all names, places, events, book titles, series titles, and all other proper nouns exactly correct and as they appear on a reputable source—e.g., the publication's website, Amazon.com, the author's website, and never Wikipedia? (*Publishers Weekly*, not *Publisher's Weekly*; *The Da Vinci Code*, not *The DaVinci Code*; Frank McCarron, not Frank Mccarron; Stephen King, not Steven King.)

- Are all major claims and facts presented by the author of the piece sound? ("More than one hundred people have..."; "Best-selling author"; "winner of the TK prize.")
- Is all quoted material ("As John Updike used to say ...") sound and properly attributed to the right speaker/author?
- Is all text excerpted from books exactly as it appears in the original work? (For many titles, you can verify with Google Books.)
- Is relevant pricing/location information correct wherever mentioned?
- If any information is unverifiable on the Web, has a reputable source (e.g., a conference organizer, an author) been contacted for verification?
- Do all links work?
- Do all numerical references add up, and are all statistics sound and properly sourced?

QUERYING MAGAZINE ARTICLES: A CHECKLIST

Speaking of checklists, here's another. Copy and print (or, heaven forbid, tear out) the following, gleaned from the "Pitch Perfect" query chapter, and tick everything off this list before you hit "Send."

BEFORE THE QUERY

- Read two to three copies of the publication, and know it well. Make sure it's the right market for your work and that you can envision your piece in it.
- Browse the publication's online archives—and those of its main competitors—to ensure they haven't recently covered the topic you're proposing.
- Find and study the publication's submission guidelines, and follow them to a T.

THE QUERY ITSELF

Make sure it ...

- is not exceedingly longer than a page.
- is written in AP Style (or the publication's preferred style), in flawless, sparkling prose.
- has a short, punchy intro, like a *logline*.
- is to the point and focused like a laser on one idea.
- matches the general tone of the publication.
- explains, whether directly or indirectly, how the story will benefit readers.
- includes a few concrete examples.
- includes a proposed word count.
- explains why you're the best person to write the piece (which could be any number of factors—an expertise, a connection, a fantastic and fresh angle, etc.).
- includes a short, relevant bio.
- includes links to clips (if you have them).
- has been edited, tightened, and polished until, frankly, you can't stand the sight of the thing.

AFTER THE QUERY

- If you haven't heard back, wait until the time frame stated in the submission guidelines has elapsed, and then send a quick, simple follow-up note.
- Regardless of whether you get accepted or rejected, be polite and thank the editor for her response. (After all, freelancing is all about building relationships and not burning bridges, even with curmudgeonly/surly editors.)
- Be sure to inquire about the publication's editorial calendar.

APPENDIX

WORDS OF WISDOM

Here I give you Marc D. Allan's "The Search for Universal Truth"—an article that manages, in a mere 800 words, to be one of the most wisdom-laden meditations I've read on the craft, and a favorite piece of mine.

THE SEARCH FOR UNIVERSAL TRUTH

Two-time Pulitzer Prize-winner Gene Weingarten shares his thoughts on writing, reporting and how, exactly, to capture the meaning of life.

By Marc D. Allan. Originally published in *Writer's Digest*, December 2011.

Gene Weingarten suggests that winning a Pulitzer Prize is "pure luck."

"The Pulitzer is a crapshoot," *The Washington Post* feature writer/humor columnist says. "Your piece has to hit a few people the right way at the right moment."

Easy for Weingarten to be modest: He's the only two-time winner of the Pulitzer for feature writing. In the first, 2008's "The Fiddler in the Subway" ("Pearls Before Breakfast" when it first appeared in *The Washington Post*), Weingarten arranged for violin virtuoso Joshua Bell to play outside a D.C. Metro station during morning rush hour to see if anyone would notice. His 2010 winner, "Fatal Distraction," recounts stories of parents who accidentally killed their children by forgetting them in cars.

Those stories and 18 others are collected in *The Fiddler in the Subway*, which includes an introduction that doubles as a superbly instructive primer on writing.

Here, the feature-writing guru offers the inside story on how he crafts his Pulitzer-grade prose.

What's the one thing an aspiring writer must understand about writing?

I can tell you what it's definitely not. It's definitely not "*I* before *e* except after *c*," because what about 'either'"?

But seriously … is there one thing an aspiring writer must understand?

That it's hard. If you think it's not hard, you're not doing it right.

One of the things I admire about your work is that you consistently prove that great writing begins with great reporting. Talk about the importance of reporting.

Well, let's start with the maxim that the best writing is understated, meaning it's not full of flourishes and semaphores and tap dancing and vocabulary dumps that get in the way of the story you are telling. Once you accept that, what are you left with? You are left with the story you are telling.

The story you are telling is only as good as the information in it: things you elicit, or things you observe, that make a narrative come alive; things that support your point not just through assertion, but through example; quotes that don't just convey information, but also personality. That's all reporting.

What distinguishes a well-told story from a poorly told one?

All of the above. Good reporting, though, requires a lot of thinking; I always counsel writers working on features to keep in mind that they are going to have to deliver a cinematic feel to their anecdotes. When you are interviewing someone, don't just write down what he says. Ask yourself: *Does this guy remind you of someone? What does the room feel like?* Notice smells, voice inflection, neighborhoods you pass through. Be a cinematographer.

Do you have any particular writing rituals or techniques that would help other writers?

Until I got to the end of your sentence, I had an answer. Alas, I don't think this would be helpful to many writers: After I report a story, I look at my notes carefully, then lock them away and don't look at them again until I have a first draft. I find it liberating to write without being chained to your notes; it helps you craft an ideal story. Then I go back to the notes and realize what I wrote that I can't really support, what quotes aren't quite as good as I thought, etc. It can be hugely frustrating, but it also sometimes leads me to go back and improve reporting, to make the story as good as I thought it could be. Not sure this will be helpful to most people. It's kind of insane.

You say all stories are ultimately about the meaning of life. How do you find that heart of the story?

By persuading yourself, going in to a story, that it must be about something larger than itself—some universal truth—and always searching for whatever that is. Sometimes, midway through, you realize it's not what you thought, it's something else. But, to quote Roseanne Rosannadanna, "... It's always something."

Let's say you only get 20 minutes with your subject. How do you find the meaning of life in 20 minutes?

Nasty question. But you gotta be fair here: I never said all stories have to explain the meaning of life. All stories have to at least try to explain some small portion of the meaning of life. You can do that in 20 minutes, and 15 inches. I still remember a piece that the great Barry Bearak did in *The Miami Herald* some 30 years ago. It was a nothing story, really: Some high school kid was leading a campaign to ban books he found offensive from the school library. Bearak didn't even have an interview with the kid, who was ducking him. The story was short, mostly about the issue.

But Bearak had a fact that he withheld until the kicker. The fact put the whole story, subtly, in complete perspective. The kicker noted the true, wonderful fact that the kid was not in school that day because "his ulcer was acting up." Meaning of life, 15 inches.

Marc D. Allan is a freelance writer based in Indianapolis.

15 THINGS A WRITER SHOULD NEVER DO

And, finally, I'll leave you with the following. It was written in about twenty minutes, but has gone on to be my most popular piece for *Writer's Digest* (besting the ones that took weeks to write and left me in search of a toupe). I attach it here, and bid you well on your writing journey.

1. DON'T ASSUME THERE IS ANY SINGLE PATH OR PLAY-BOOK WRITERS NEED TO FOLLOW. (Or, for that matter, a definitive superlative list of Dos and Don'ts ...) Simply put: You have to do what works best for you. Listen to the voices in your head, and learn to train and trust them. More often than not, they'll let you

THE ESSENTIAL GUIDE TO FREELANCE WRITING

know if you're on the right path. People often bemoan the surplus of contradictory advice in the writing world—but it's there because there really is no yellow brick road, and a diversity of perspectives allows you to cherry-pick what uniquely suits you and your abilities.

2. **DON'T TRY TO WRITE LIKE YOUR IDOLS.** Be yourself. Yeah, it sounds a bit cheesy, but it's true: The one thing you've got that no one else has is your own voice, your own style, your own approach. Use it. (If you try to write like anyone else, your readers will know.) Perhaps author Allegra Goodman said it best: "Know your literary tradition, savor it, steal from it, but when you sit down to write, forget about worshiping greatness and fetishizing masterpieces."

3. **DON'T GET TOO SWEPT UP IN DEBATES ABOUT OUTLINING/NOT OUTLINING, WHETHER OR NOT YOU SHOULD *WRITE WHAT YOU KNOW*,** whether or not you should edit as you go along or at the end. Again, just experiment and do what works best for you. The freedom that comes with embracing this approach is downright cathartic.

4. **DON'T PUT ALL YOUR EGGS IN ONE BASKET WHEN IT COMES TO PITCHING SOMETHING**—always be working on your next article or idea while you're querying. Keeping your creative side in gear while focusing on the business of selling your work prevents bigger stalls in your writing life down the road.

5. **DON'T BE UNNECESSARILY DISHONEST, RUDE, HOSTILE**—people in the publishing industry talk, and word spreads about who's great to work with and who's not. As I said earlier in the book, publishing is a big business, but it's a pretty incestuous business. Keep those family reunions gossip-free.

6. **DON'T EVER HATE SOMEONE FOR THE FEEDBACK THEY GIVE YOU.** No piece of writing is universally beloved. Nearly every beta reader, editor, or agent will have a different opinion of your work, and there's value in that. Accept what nuggets you believe are valid, recognize the recurring issues you might want or need to address, and toss the edits your gut tells you to toss. (If the changes are mandatory for a deal, however, you'll need to do

224

some deeper soul-searching.) Be open to criticism—it will make you a better writer.

7. **... BUT, DON'T BE SUSCEPTIBLE TO THE BARBS OF ON-LINE TROLLS**—you know, those people who post sociopathic comments for the sake of posting sociopathic comments.

8. **DON'T EVER LOWER YOU GUARD WHEN IT COMES TO THE BASICS:**[1] Good spelling, healthy mechanics, sound grammar. They are the foundations that keep our writing houses from imploding ... and our queries from hitting the recycling bin before our stories can speak for themselves.

9. **DON'T EVER WRITE SOMETHING IN AN ATTEMPT TO SATISFY A MARKET TREND AND MAKE A QUICK BUCK.** By the time such a book is ready to go, the trend will likely have passed. The astronomical amount of romantic teenage vampire novels in desk drawers is more than a nuisance—it's a wildfire hazard. Write the story that gives you insomnia.

10. **DON'T BE SPITEFUL ABOUT ANOTHER WRITER'S SUCCESS.** Celebrate it. As author Amy Sue Nathan recalled when detailing her path to publication in the July/August 2013 issue of WD: "Writers I knew were landing book deals and experiencing other things I was working toward, so I made a decision to learn from them instead of begrudging them. I learned that another author's success doesn't infringe on mine."

11. **DON'T EVER ASSUME IT'S EASY.** Writers with one book on shelves or one story in print often had to keep stacking up unpublished manuscripts until they could reach the publisher's doorbell. (The exception being those lucky nineteen-year-old savants you sometimes hear about, or, say, Snooki. But, hey, success still isn't guaranteed—after all, Snooki's *Gorilla Beach: A Novel* has only sold 3,445 copies.) Success is one of those things that's often damn near impossible to accurately predict unless you already have it in spades.

---

1 Yes, the missing r was intentional. Though I still got trolled for it when this piece originally ran online, of course.

12. DON'T FORGET TO GET OUT ONCE IN A WHILE. Writing is a reflection of real life. It's all too easy to sit too long at that desk and forget to live.

13. DON'T EVER DISCOUNT THE SHEER TEACHING POWER (AND THERAPEUTIC GOODNESS) OF A GREAT READ. The makeshift MFA program of countless writers has been a well-stocked bookshelf.

14. DON'T BE AFRAID TO GIVE UP ... ON A PARTICULAR PIECE. Sometimes a story just doesn't work, and you shouldn't spend years languishing on something you just can't fix. (After all, you can always come back to it later, right?)

15. BUT, DON'T EVER *REALLY* GIVE UP. Writers write. It's what we do. It's what we have to do. Sure, we can all say over a half-empty bottle of wine that we're going to throw the towel in this time, but let's be honest: Very few of us ever do. And none of us are ever really all that surprised when we find ourselves back at our computers, tapping away, and waiting for that electric, amazing moment when the pebble of a story shakes loose and begins to skitter down that great hill. ...

ABOUT
THE AUTHOR

Zachary Petit is a freelance writer and the editor in chief of *Print*, a seventy-five-year-old National Magazine Award-winning publication about graphic design and culture. Formerly he was the senior managing editor of *HOW* magazine, *Print*, and *Writer's Digest* and executive editor of such newsstand titles as *Writing Basics*, *Writer's Yearbook*, and *Writer's Workbook*.

During his tenure at *Print*, the publication won Best Consumer Magazine in the Folio: Eddie & Ozzie Awards, the industry's biggest competition.

Alongside the thousands of articles he has penned as a staff writer and editor, covering everything from the secret lives of mall Santas to creative legends, his words regularly appear in *National Geographic Kids* and have also popped up in the pages of *National Geographic*, Melissa Rossi's What Every American Should Know book series, *McSweeney's Internet Tendency*, and many other outlets. He is the co-author, alongside Brian A. Klems, of *A Year of Writing Prompts: 366 Story Ideas for Honing Your Craft and Eliminating Writer's Block*.

Petit lives in the Midwest, never tires of defending the region to New Yorkers, and is forever slightly uncomfortable referring to himself in the third person.

COLOPHON

Thank you to *Writer's Digest* for long giving me a place to ramble, and to my editor, Rachel Randall, for putting up with all my footnotes and for not throwing the book in the WD fireplace.

To M, for allowing me to be a delinquent husband for a couple of months as I wrote this. (And for being the best.)

To Mom and Dad, for supporting my exceedingly strange career aspirations, and for not sending me to military school as threatened.

To R, for being my fearless fellow world traveler and the best sister one could have.

To J, for being my creative partner over so many strange times and strange years.

To Melissa Rossi, who took a chance on me and taught me that nonfiction need not be boring.

And finally, and perhaps most important, thank you, dear reader, for listening. Have questions? Contact me at zacharypetit.com, or give me a shout on Twitter: @ZacharyPetit. It may take me a moment, but I'll write back.

INDEX